INDIA-PAKISTAN COMPOSITE DIALOGUE PROCESS

INDIA-PAKISTAN COMPOSITE DIALOGUE PROCESS

Issues and Action

Sajad Padder

KALPAZ

ISBN: 978-93-5128-086-6

Price : ₹ 540

First Published, 2015

Published by

Kalpaz Publications
C-30, Satyawati Nagar,
Delhi – 110052
E-mail: kalpaz@hotmail.com
Ph.: 9212142040

Laser Typesetting: Gyan Print (AB-I)
Printed at: G. Print Process, Delhi

Cataloging in Publication Data—DK
Courtesy: D.K. Agencies (P) Ltd. <docinfo@dkagencies.com>

Padder, Sajad Ahmad, author.
India-Pakistan composite dialogue process : issues and action / Sajad Ahmad Padder.
pages cm
Includes bibliographical references (pages).
ISBN 9789351280866

1. India—Foreign relations—Pakistan. 2. Pakistan—Foreign relations—India. I. Title.

DDC 327.5405491 23

Contents

Preface

The India-Pakistan peace process, technically known as the 'Composite Dialogue Process' (CDP), has sailed through numerous highs and lows in bilateral relations since 1997. It has remained susceptible to unforeseen incidents which have derailed it several times in the past. However, since April 2003, it has proceeded steadily till the Mumbai terror attacks of November 26, 2008 when the dialogue process was suspended for an unforeseen future. This book dwells on the history of the peace process since its inception in 1997 and examines the progress made in the eight baskets of issues namely: Peace and Security Confidence Building Measures; Jammu and Kashmir; Siachen; Sir Creek; Wullar Barrage/ Tulbul Navigation Project; Terrorism and Drug Trafficking; Economic and Commercial Co-operation: and Promotion of Friendly Exchanges in various fields. The analysis of the peace process in this book hinges on several key questions. First, how is the Composite Dialogue different from other dialogues held between India and Pakistan? Second, what are the main achievements of the Composite Dialogue Process? Third, has this dialogue process helped in changing mindset and bridging the trust deficit between the two countries? And fourth, what are the prospects of resolving the bilateral issues through the Composite Dialogue Process? The book is divided into following five chapters. Chapter-I deals with the "Brief Survey of Indo-Pak Relations in the Context of War and Peace Treaties". It highlights the factors that have led to the straining of relations between the two countries since 1947 and the major agreements reached upon to resolve the bilateral disputes. Chapter-II deals with the "Issues and Components in the Composite Dialogue Process." Chapter-III focuses on "Mapping the Progress of the Composite Dialogue Process." Chapter-IV highlights the "Challenges to the Composite Dialogue Process." And finally Chapter-V sums up the main "Conclusions" of the study.

My heartfelt thanks go to my teacher and guide Professor Gull Mohd Wani, Director, UNESCO Madanjeet Singh Institute of Kashmir Studies, University of Kashmir, Srinagar, for his consistent guidance, affection and encouragement. Prof Wani's incisive feedback and conceptual inputs have been of great help. I am also grateful to Prof Noor Ahmad Baba, former Head of the Department of Political Science, University of Kashmir for cheerfully helping me out in times of need.

I am obliged to Aziz Ahmed Khan, the former High Commissioner of Pakistan to India for sharing his valuable insights on the dialogue process. I am also grateful to Dr Hamida Nayeem, Head of Department of English, University of Kashmir and Dr Mehboob Beig, Member Parliament, (Lok Sabha), for sharing their views on the subject. I am highly thankful to the faculty and staff members in the Department of Political Science, University of Kashmir Srinagar for their umpteen help and care.

I am indebted to my parents, who in spite of being illiterate, have reinforced my will to undertake the study and initially provided with the much needed financial support.

I dedicate this book to my late younger sister, Shugufta Bashir, who left me deserted after her sudden death in the year 2006.

Sajad Ahmad Padder

List of Abbreviations

AFSPA	Armed Forces Special Powers Act
AGPL	Actual Ground Position Line
ANF	Anti Narcotic Force
APHC	All Parties Hurriyat Conference
BJP	Bharatiya Janata Party
CBM's	Confidence Building Measures
CDP	Composite Dialogue Process
CFL	Cease-fire Line
CI	Counter Insurgency
DAA	Disturbed Areas Act
DGMOs	Director General of Military Operations
EEZ	Exclusive Economic Zone
FATA	Federally-Administered Tribal Areas
GI	Geographical Indication
GSK	Glaxo Smith Kline
IAF	Indian Air Force
IB	International Border
ICP	Integrated Check-Post

IDSA	Institute for Defence Studies and Analyses
IPI	Iran-Pakistan-India
IPJC	India-Pakistan Joint Commission
ISI	Inter-Services Intelligence
IWT	Indus Water Treaty
JATM	Joint Anti-terrorism Mechanism
JI	Jamaat-e-Islami
JKLF	Jammu and Kashmir Liberation Front
JSG	Joint Study Group
JWG	Joint Working Group
LoC	Line of Control
MAF	Million Acre Feet
MFN	Most Favoured Nation
MHS	Mutually Hurting Stalemate
MoU	Memorandum of Understanding
NC	National Conference
NCB	Narcotics Control Bureau
NTBs	Non-Tariff Barriers
NWFP	Northwest Frontier Province
PDP	Peoples Democratic Party
PILDAT	Pakistan Institute of Legislative Development and Transparency
PML-N	Pakistan Muslim League-Nawaz
PNE	Peaceful Nuclear Device

RCN	Red Corner Notices
RTC	Round Table Conference
SAARC	South Asian Association for Regional Cooperation
SAFTA	South Asian Free Trade Agreement
TNP	Tulbul Navigation Project
TOR	Terms of Reference
UJC	United Jihad Council
UN	United Nations
UNCIP	United Nations Commission for India and Pakistan
UNCLOS	United Nations Convention on Laws of the Sea
UNMOGIP	United Nations Military Observer Group in India and Pakistan

1

Brief Survey of Indo-Pak Relations in the Context of War and Peace Treaties

Birth of Pakistan

Until the arrival of Muslim traders, missionaries, and armies in the late seventh and early eighth centuries, the population of South Asia was primarily Hindu and Buddhist. By A.D. 1100 a number of Indo-Muslim states had been established, and by the sixteenth century the Mughal Empire dominated the northern India. The British formally disbanded the empire in 1858, at which time about one-quarter of India's population were Muslims. They were concentrated in East Bengal, the Northwest Frontier, Punjab, Sindh, and Baluchistan, with large Muslim minorities in present-day Uttar Pradesh and Madhya Pradesh.[1] India's Muslims slowly adapted to British rule yet maintained their identity by establishing the Aligarh Muslim University in 1875. Indian National Congress, spearheaded by Mohandas Karamchand Gandhi and Jawaharlal Nehru, sought a unified country built around the principles of secularism and liberal democracy. Although the majority of the Congress Party membership came from the mainstream Hindu population, the party embodied all major ethnic groups of India and had a vision of a state not supporting any single religion.[2] Many Muslim leaders were wary of majority rule and demanded safeguards by way of separate electorates. In order to press for their demands with the colonial rulers, they formed the Muslim League Party in December 1906. Their claim for separate electorates was accepted by the British in the Government of India Act of 1909, which offered limited political rights to the Indian subjects. The British rulers were sympathetic to separate constituencies for Muslims which they hoped would weaken the incipient nationalist movement, spearheaded by the Congress Party. However, over time this policy helped to unify the Muslim community in a communal and political sense and sowed the seeds for the idea of Pakistan. Although the Congress Party initially accepted separate Muslim electorates in 1916, it subsequently rejected the idea in the constitutional proposals it made in 1928. Alienation from both the British and the Congress Party led to the proposal for a separate Muslim homeland by the League, which was first put forward by the poet Muhammad Iqbal in 1930.[3] Three years later a group of Indian students at Cambridge proposed naming it Pakistan. As the prospects of British withdrawal from South Asia increased, the Muslim League, led by lawyer-politician Mohammad Ali Jinnah, declared its support for the Idea of Pakistan at its 1940 Lahore session. One year later the most powerful of the religious Islamist groups, the Jama'at-Islami, was founded.

Following negotiations between the British, the secular but largely Hindu Indian National Congress, and the Muslim League in 1946, the state of Pakistan was born on August 14, 1947, and India gained Independence on August 15. Pakistan was carved out of five provinces of British India plus some princely states. Under the new boundaries, the provinces of Bengal and Punjab were partitioned and millions of people had to move. The eastern part of Bengal, which was overwhelmingly Muslim, became East Pakistan. Western Punjab, including the important princely state of Bahawalpur, became the Pakistani province of Punjab. The eastern area, and a number of ethnically Punjabi princely states, became the Indian part of Punjab. West Pakistan also included Baluchistan, the Northwest Frontier Province (NWFP), and Sindh.[4]

The Emergence of Kashmir as a Problem

The Indian Independence Act of 1947 contained a provision that the 562 princely states scattered throughout the subcontinent and partially autonomous under British rule, had the option to join either India or Pakistan. With the strenuous efforts of Sardar Vallabhai Patel, almost all states within India joined the Indian Union while Jinnah succeeded in gaining the accession by the Muslim princes within Pakistan's territorial domain.[5] Three princely states decided to stay independent from both India and Pakistan: Jammu and Kashmir in the north, Hyderabad in the south, and Junagadh in the west. While the rulers of the latter two were Muslim, the majority of their population was Hindu and their accession to India occurred through internal revolt or Indian police actions.

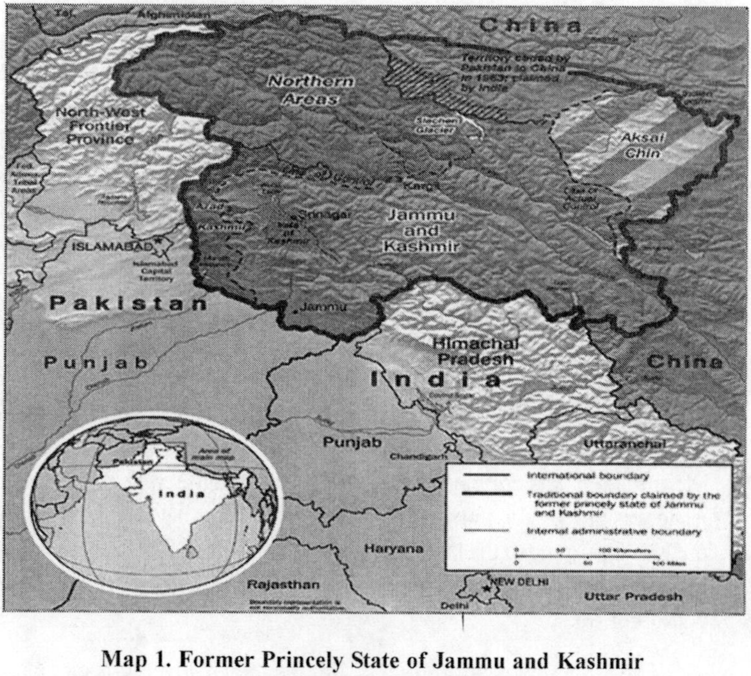

Map 1. Former Princely State of Jammu and Kashmir and the Adjoining Areas.

Courtesy of the University of Texas Libraries, The University of Texas at Austin.

New Delhi legitimised these accessions through subsequent popular referenda.[6] Only Jammu and Kashmir emerged as the most contentious, given its geographical proximity to Pakistan and a majority Muslim population even as a substantial Hindu population inhabited the Jammu area and a Buddhist population lived in the Ladakh region. Situated in the northeast of the Indian subcontinent, the state of Jammu and Kashmir occupied a territory of 222,800 sq. km.[7] Comparable in size to Great Britain, it was one of the largest states in India. It consisted of the Valley in the centre, encircled by the regions-clockwise from north—-Gilgit, Baltistan, Ladakh, Jammu and Poonch. Its neighbours were Afghanistan to the north-west, China's Sinkiang Province to the north, Tibet to the east, and British India to the South.

The Hindu ruler of Kashmir, Maharaja Hari Singh, first chose to remain independent from both India and Pakistan, but in reaction to an invasion in October 1947 by tribal forces from Pakistan's Northwest Frontier Province (which were aided by Pakistani regular troops), he sought India's help. Following his signing an agreement to accede to India and the approval of Kashmir's undisputed leader of the time, Sheikh Mohammad Abdullah, the Indian forces intervened and managed to partially evict the intruders. Jinnah's decision to send in Pakistani troops escalated the conflict to a war between the two states, which lasted until the end of 1948. The continuation of the conflict and tension between the two countries led them to begin an arms race leading to consolidate the influence of their national security institutions. Lord Mountbatten held a meeting with Jinnah at Lahore in November 1947 to solve the controversy over Kashmir, but failed. Again, on 8th December a meeting of the Joint Defence Council was held at Lahore in which Nehru and Mountbatten participated. But it could not solve the issue of Kashmir and Lord Mountbatten was convinced that a negotiated settlement of the Kashmir issue was practically impossible. Nehru and Mountbatten decided to refer the Kashmir issue to the UN, but Sardar Patel did not like the idea. He tried his best to stop Nehru from referring the Kashmir issue to the U.N. but could not do so.[8]

The India–Pakistan conflict is, simultaneously over territory, national identity, and power position in the region. The political status of Kashmir, from Pakistan's perspective, is the unfinished business of the partition of the subcontinent on a religious basis in 1947. Successive Pakistani leaders have viewed the gaining of the entire Jammu and Kashmir state from Indian control as their core national mission for identity and strategic reasons.[9] To the Pakistanis, the Indian–controlled Muslim-majority state of Kashmir, if given full freedom to choose in a plebiscite, would join Pakistan. However, this state-centered, legalistic interpretation of the 'right to self-determination' is significantly different from the highly populist version articulated by proponents of an independent Kashmir.[10] The Jammu and Kashmir National Conference (NC) stands for 'greater autonomy', while the People's Democratic Party (PDP) strives for 'self-rule'. The All Parties Hurriyat Conference (APHC) stands for plebiscite and the inclusion of Kashmiris in the talks between India and Pakistan for the final settlement of the Kashmir dispute. Thus, despite the preference of most Kashmiri nationalist groups for independence or greater autonomy from both countries, Pakistan steadfastly holds the view that the partition of the sub-continent is still incomplete and that Pakistan's Islamic identity will not be total until the territory is unified with that country.[11]

From India's standpoint, besides being an integral part of India legally by virtue of the instrument of accession signed by Maharaja, Kashmir is very much a part of the nation's secular identity. To New Delhi, partition was completed in 1947 and no further territorial concessions to Pakistan are feasible. Further, India argues that the several democratic elections that it has held, have legitimised the accession. The presence of more than 138 million (approx.14.2 per cent of the total) strong Muslim population in India attests to the Indian belief that partition on the basis of religion was an unfortunate historical *fait accompli* and that ceding Jammu and Kashmir, or even portions of the Kashmir Valley or the Vale of Kashmir, where the Muslims constitute a majority, to Pakistan would result in a second partition, negating India's secular credentials. India's fear is that letting Kashmir go could open the floodgates of separatist movements in other parts of India and that it would be followed by inter-communal violence reminiscent of the partition days. There exists no serious constituency in India from the left to the right that believes that Kashmir should be ceded to Pakistan.[12] Extreme right-wingers in the Bharatiya Janata Party (BJP) would want to forcefully integrate Kashmir and even recover the portion held by Pakistan (Azad Kashmir), since ceding it to Pakistan or allowing independence to Kashmiri's will be tantamount to placating the minority Muslims, while more moderate political groups would like to see a peaceful integration of Kashmir within the Indian Union. It seems restoring Kashmir's pre-1953 autonomous status is the maximum concession that most Indian moderates would agree to.[13]

Despite the rhetoric about the indivisibility of Kashmir, it seems that the Indian elite and public could live with the status quo on the territorial division, i.e., acceptance of the Line of Control separating the Indian and Pakistani sides of Kashmir as the permanent border.[14] However, even in this instance, compromise has been constrained by the disparate positions within the Kashmiri liberation movement. The movement is conglomerate of groups, some want to create an Islamic state while others are more tolerant towards the inclusion of the minority Hindu and Buddhist populations. The involvement of Islamic insurgent groups from Pakistan, Afghanistan, and other parts of the Middle East and Central Asia and the deadly terrorist tactics they employ have undermined their cause within India. In the post-September 11, 2001 context, they have lost much international sympathy. Despite this, the fact remains that a peace settlement between India and Pakistan would require the fulfillment of Kashmiri aspirations in some meaningful way. The challenge remains how the three mutually exclusive claims of India, Pakistan, and the Kashmiri movement can be accommodated, satisfying the aspirations of the three contestants simultaneously.

Kashmir in the UN

On 1st January, 1948 the Indian representative to the UN, P. P. Pillai brought to the notice of the Security Council under Article 35 of the UN Charter, a situation in the State of Jammu and Kashmir, the continuance of which was likely to endanger the maintenance of international peace and security.[15] The Security Council adopted resolution 39 (1948), establishing the United Nations Commission for India and Pakistan (UNCIP) to investigate and mediate the dispute. In April 1948, by its resolution 47(1948), the Council decided to enlarge the membership of UNCIP and to recommend various measures including the use of observers to stop the fighting. At the recommendation of UNCIP, the Secretary-General appointed the Military Adviser to support the Commission on military aspects and provided for a group of military observers to assist him. The first team of unarmed military observers, which eventually formed the nucleus of the United Nations Military Observer Group in India and Pakistan (UNMOGIP), arrived in the mission area in January 1949 to supervise in the State of Jammu and Kashmir the ceasefire between India and Pakistan and to assist the Military Adviser to UNCIP. The tasks of the observers, as defined by the Military Adviser, were to accompany the local authorities in their investigations, gather as much information as possible, and report as completely, accurately and impartially as possible. Any direct intervention by the observers between the opposing parties or any interference in the armies' orders was to be avoided. These arrangements remained in effect until the conclusion of the Karachi Agreement on 27 July, 1949 establishing a ceasefire line to be supervised by UN military observers.[16]

Karachi Agreement—1949

The Karachi Agreement signed by India and Pakistan on the 27th of July, 1949 specified that UNCIP would station observers where it deemed necessary, and that the ceasefire line would be verified mutually on the ground by local commanders on each side with the assistance of UN military observers. Disagreements were to be referred to the UNCIP Military Adviser, whose decision would be final.

The Agreement was signed by the following:

1. Honourable Mushtaq Ahmed Gurmani, Minister without Portfolio, Government of Pakistan.
2. Sardar Mohammed Ibrahim Khan, the president of Azad Kashmir .
3. Choudhry Ghulam Abbas, Head of All Jammu and Kashmir Muslim Conference.[17]

The UNCIP submitted three interim reports. In the third interim report it suggested that as the military situation had changed, the task of solving the entire issue be entrusted to one person who would act as a mediator instead of a Commission.[18] On the recommendations of the Commission the Security Council appointed its president, General McNaughton as mediator. He forwarded various proposals to India and Pakistan which could not make a breakthrough and on 12 April, 1950, the Security Council appointed Owen Dixon of Australia to implement McNaughton's proposals for the demilitarisation of state, but he too failed. On 15 September, 1950, Dixon submitted his report, suggesting the partition of Kashmir rather than holding an overall plebiscite.[19] Dixon's proposals were not acceptable to both India and Pakistan. The discussion on Kashmir issue was once again resumed in the Security Council in 21 February, 1951 with the submission of a joint draft resolution by the UK and the US. Presenting the draft resolution Gladwyn Jebb of the UK submitted that "no reference to the wishes of Kashmir regarding the future accession of that state made otherwise than under the auspices and with the full consent of the UN can be regarded as constituting a settlement acceptable to this Council."[20] This Anglo-American reaction was the result of India's policy of going ahead with a Constituent Assembly in Kashmir. Another revised draft resolution was introduced after hearing the views of Indian and Pakistani representatives. Pakistan agreed to accept the resolution while Nehru considered it as "extraordinarily objectionable".[21] Again at the 542 meeting of the Security Council, Frank P. Graham, Senator from North Carolina, US was appointed UN representative for India and Pakistan. He submitted five reports and suggested direct negotiation between India and Pakistan.[22]

Delhi Agreement—-1952

In order to try and resolve the issue of Jammu and Kashmir's relationship with the Indian union, the Indian Government invited leaders from the State to New Delhi for talks. On 17th June, 1952, a delegation headed by Mirza Afzal Beg (then Revenue Minister) arrived in the Indian capital. Sheikh Abdullah and other prominent National Conference leaders joined the talks a month later. On 24th July, 1952 the two sides reached a consensus in what became known as the Delhi Agreement.[23] According to the terms of the agreement Jammu and Kashmir was part of India, but it would at the same time retain a high degree of autonomy. Thus, for instance while retaining Article 370 and having their Sadar-i-Riyasat chosen by the State Assembly rather than appointed by the Indian President as in other states, Kashmiris would be classified as citizens of India and their flag would take second place to the Indian tricolour.[24] Having signed the Delhi Agreement, both Abdullah and the Indian government proceeded to abuse it, the former by persisting with calls for independence, the latter by asserting its authority beyond the spheres allocated to it. In his opening address to the Constituent Assembly, Sheikh Abdullah had ruled out independence on the grounds that as a small state Jammu and Kashmir would be vulnerable to outside aggression. To quote him:

> 'We have to consider the alternative of making ourselves an Eastern Switzerland, of keeping aloof from both States [India and Pakistan], but having friendly relations with them. This may seem attractive in that it would appear to pave the way out of the present deadlock. To us as a tourist country, it could also have certain obvious advantages. But in considering independence we must not ignore practical considerations. First, it is not easy to protect sovereignty and independence in a small country which has not sufficient strength to defend itself on our long and difficult frontiers bordering so many countries. Secondly, we do not find powerful guarantors among them to pull together always in assuring us freedom from aggression.'[25]

But Abdullah's actions subsequent to this made it clear that he still considered independence a possibility. In order to overcome the aforementioned obstacle to independence, he attempted to find a powerful 'backer' who could protect an independent Jammu and Kashmir. The main target of his efforts was the United States. In a meeting with Loy Henderson, US Ambassador to India, on 29 September, 1950, Sheikh Abdullah made clear not only his own desire for independence, but further claimed that this was what the majority of the State's population wanted, and even that those in Azad Kashmir would join an independent state.[26] However, he acknowledged this could only be possible with US or UN assistance. Abdullah also attempted to win Australian backing when he met Walter Crocker, the High Commissioner for Australia, in 1952.[27] The Indian Government was not unaware of the nature of Abdullah's discussions with foreign leaders, but after July 1952, they were confident that the independence issue had been buried once and for all. However, in May 1953, less than a year after signing the Delhi Agreement, Abdullah was again discussing independence, this time with Adlai Stevenson, US Presidential candidate. For India this was 'the straw that broke the camel's back'; far from being the loyal ally they had expected when they put him in power, Abdullah had become a liability who had to be removed. On the other hand, small scale protests against Abdullah's government had been going on for some time in Jammu mainly through a party formed by Bal Raj Madhok in 1947, the Praja Parishad. Its main demands were the abrogation of Article 370 and the complete merger of Jammu and Kashmir with India. The Praja Parishad's anti-autonomy views were succinctly expressed in a popular slogan:[28]

> Two constitutions in one country, two flags, two Heads of State, these will not be accepted. *(Ekdeshmein do vidhaan, ekdeshmein do nishaan, ekdeshmein do pradhaan: nahinchalenge, nahinchalenge*).

The Praja Parishad movement received strong encouragement from Hindu groups within India, notably from Jana Sangh. Formed by Shyama Prasad Mookerjee in 1951, one of the four points for strengthening Indian unity listed in its first manifesto was the full integration of Jammu and Kashmir into the Indian Union.[29] In November, 1952 two of the Praja Parishad's leaders, Prem Nath Dogra and Sham Lal Sharma, were arrested. Hindu anger, already aroused by these arrests, was inflamed by the arrest of Shyama Prasad Mookerjee on 8 May 1953 after he attempted to enter the state, and his subsequent death (of a heart-attack) in detention.[30]

Removal of Sheikh Abdullah—1953

Public pressure on the Indian Government mounted after the pro-integration demonstrations in Jammu and Ladakh, and became irresistible after Mookerjee's death in Kashmiri detention. By exploiting a split in the National Conference leadership, New Delhi was able to engineer an internal coup and replace Sheikh Abdullah with Bakshi Ghulam Muhammad, the then Deputy Prime Minister.[31] Around midnight of the night of 8/9 August, 1953 Abdullah was duly arrested in Gulmarg, where he had gone for the weekend, and taken to Udhampur. The pretext of his arrest was that he had gone to Gulmarg to meet an emissary of Pakistan—such a meeting 'would constitute a grave danger to the State'. Bakshi was sworn in as Prime Minister by Karan Singh (Sadar-i-Riyasat) on the morning of 9 August, 1953. Karan Singh, unlike his father was strongly committed to Jammu and Kashmir joining India as an integral part. From 1953 to 1956, India and Pakistan tried to solve the dispute through direct negotiations. From 27 August, 1953 to 24 September, 1954 the Prime Ministers of India and Pakistan were in correspondence with each other. But the US military aid to Pakistan changed the whole context of the Kashmir issue. It changed the climate of the sub-continent so much so that bilateral negotiations were unthinkable. India also changed her attitude as Sheikh Abdullah on whose support her entire policy had hitherto been based, changed his policy. He was dismissed from the Prime Minister-ship and put in jail because he had begun to talk in terms of independence for Kashmir.[32]

The debate on Kashmir resumed in the UN Security Council in 1954 and continued from 761 to 775 meetings, but nothing tangible came out. Two draft resolutions were also introduced. The famous Four Powers resolution was tabled by Australia, Cuba, the UK and the US on 14 February 1957 in the 768 meeting of the Security Council. It was voted with 10 in favour and the USSR against. The US representative Barco accused the USSR for her veto. He said "the action of the Soviet Union can have only one purpose, to perpetuate international conflict and dissentions between two of Asia's great countries."[33] At the 774 meeting on 21 February 1957, the Council adopted an amended resolution with ten votes in favour, none against and one abstention, calling upon its president, Gunnar Jarring of Sweden to discuss with the Indian and Pakistani Governments any proposals which they deemed fit for the settlement of the Kashmir issue having regard to the previous resolutions of the UN. In the report which he submitted on 29th April, 1957, he observed that if a plebiscite would be held 'grave problems might arise'. He indicated the apprehension of communal passions that might arise in the subcontinent by a plebiscite irrespective of the result.[34] The Jarring report was received with satisfaction in India. The Indian press placed special emphasis on his reference to the "changing, political, economic and strategic factors surrounding the whole of Kashmir question". Another resolution was adopted at the 808 meeting of the Council on 2nd December, 1957 which requested Frank P. Graham to make any recommendation to the parties for further appropriate action for the implementation of the UN resolutions. He submitted his report on 28th March, 1958, suggesting a conference at the Prime Ministers level. The suggestion was accepted by Pakistan but rejected by India. When Field Marshal Ayub Khan became the President of Pakistan in 1958, it was felt that the situation might change.

Indus Water Treaty—1960

The waters of the Indus basin begin in the Himalayan Mountains in the state of Jammu and Kashmir. They flow from the hills through the arid states of Punjab and Sindh, converging in Pakistan and emptying into the Arabian Sea, south of Karachi. Where once there was only a narrow strip of irrigated land along these rivers, developments over the last century have created a large network of canals and storage facilities that provide water for more than 26 million acres-—the largest irrigated area of any one river system in the world.[35] The partition of British India created a conflict over the plentiful waters of the Indus basin. The newly formed states were at odds over how to share and manage what was essentially a cohesive and unitary network of irrigation. Furthermore, the geography of partition was such that the Source Rivers of the Indus basin were in India. Pakistan felt its livelihood threatened by the prospect of Indian control over the tributaries that fed water into the Pakistani portion of the basin. While India certainly had its own ambitions for the profitable development of the basin, Pakistan felt acutely threatened by a conflict over the main source of water for its cultivable land. During the first years of partition the waters of the Indus were apportioned by the Inter-Dominion Accord of May 4, 1948. This accord required India to release sufficient waters to the Pakistani regions of the basin in return for annual payments from the government of Pakistan. The accord was meant to meet immediate requirements and was followed by negotiations for a more permanent solution. Neither side, however, was willing to compromise their respective positions nor did negotiations reach a stalemate. From the Indian point of view, there was nothing that Pakistan could do to prevent India from any of the schemes to divert the flow of water in the rivers. Pakistan wanted to take the matter to the International Court of Justice but India refused, arguing that the conflict required a bilateral resolution. By 1951, the two sides were no longer meeting and the situation seemed intractable. The Pakistani press was calling for more drastic action and the deadlock contributed to hostility with India. As one anonymous Indian official said at the time, "India and Pakistan can go on shouting on Kashmir for all time to come, but an early settlement on the Indus waters is essential for maintenance of peace in the sub-continent"[36]. Despite the unwillingness to compromise, both nations were anxious to find a solution, fully aware that the Indus conflict could lead to overt hostilities if unresolved. David Lilienthal, former chairman of the Tennessee Valley Authority and a former Chairman of Atomic Energy Commission, USA visited the two countries in 1951 and proposed that India and Pakistan work out a programme jointly to develop and operate the Indus Basin river system. Inspired by this idea, Eugene R. Black, then President of the World Bank, visited the two countries and proposed a Working Party of Indian, Pakistani, and World Bank engineers to tackle the functional aspects of water sharing. The two countries accepted this mediation and the World Bank stepped in with its own draft proposals for resolution in February 1954, distributing the three Eastern Rivers to India and the three Western rivers to Pakistan. Protracted talks were held amid mounting tensions, and finally the Indus Waters Treaty was signed by Jawaharlal Nehru, then Prime Minister of India; Field Marshal Ayub Khan, then President of Pakistan; and W.A.B. Illif, then President of the World Bank, in Karachi in September 1960.[37] The IWT provided for one of the most comprehensive dispute resolution mechanisms. Under the IWT, India can undertake projects on the western rivers for general conservation, flood control, irrigation and hydropower generation, and duly inform Pakistan of the same. Pakistan's objection would render it a matter of dispute to be settled either by negotiations or by a neutral expert, or by arbitration.[38] Three members, one from India, one from Pakistan and the third member by mutual agreement or an International Court of Justice appointee *in lieu* would be the arbitrators. Any unresolved 'question' between the two parties through the Permanent Indus Commission becomes a 'difference' to be referred to a neutral expert, who is appointed by the two countries, and failing that, the World Bank. If the neutral expert's recommendations are unacceptable to either of the parties, the matter would be treated as a 'dispute' and it would be referred to a Court of Arbitration established by the World Bank, along with other institutions such as the secretary general of the United Nations.[39]

Sino-Indian War of 1962 and its Impact on Indo-Pak Relations

Relations between India and Pakistan again strained after the Sino-Indian war of 1962 when the situation in the Indian sub-continent changed completely. The Indo-US relations started improving and the Sino-Pak ties were further strengthened. Pakistan condemned India for attacking China. When the firing was going on, the *Dawn*, Pakistani newspaper wrote: "China is already teaching them how foolish and costly the dreams of conquest can prove. And this is only the beginning of the story."[40] It was observed that if there would have been the slightest sympathy from Pakistan for India, then there would have been a wave of goodwill for Pakistan all over India. Again direct negotiations between India and Pakistan started at the ministerial level on the Kashmir issue. There were six rounds of talks from December 1962 to May 1963. In the meanwhile, on 2nd March 1963, the Sino-Pak Border Agreement was signed in Peking by the Foreign Ministers of China and Pakistan.[41] The India Government strongly condemned the agreement. On 2nd March, 1963 in a protest to China, New Delhi described it as an act of direct interference by the Peking Government in Indo-Pak relations. The agreement manifested the Peking Government's desire to exploit the differences between India and Pakistan on the Kashmir issue. The Indian Government blamed the Government of China for intending to destroy the amity which had been developed between India and Pakistan, as a result of the joint talks between the two countries on Kashmir and other related matters.[42] Some new developments took place during 1964, i.e. release of Sheikh Abdullah and death of Nehru. In the same year, Sheikh Abdullah visited Pakistan and found desire on the part of the President Ayub Khan for friendship with India.[43]

The Kutch Conflict—1965

The Kutch episode in April-May, 1965 worsened the Indo-Pak relations which had cooled down in 1964. A dispute arose over disagreements regarding the border in the Rann of Kutch (a 20,000 sq. km. salt marsh). Limited hostilities took place between India and Pakistan after each side accused the other of crossing what they respectively regarded as the international boundary. The monsoons intervened before the situation became too serious, and both sides accepted a British-mediated ceasefire.[44] It has been suggested that the Rann of Kutch affair was a reconnaissance exercise engaged in by both sides to gain some idea of the other's military strength and resolve.[45]

Second Kashmir War—1965

Since by 1965, all attempts at peacefully resolving the Kashmir dispute had failed, this interpretation would certainly correlate with the view that both sides had decided on a military solution. The Pakistani plan for such a military solution consisted of two stages. Rather than attack India directly, in the first stage Kashmiris themselves would be encouraged to rise against them. This encouragement would come from Pakistanis and Azad Kashmiris who would infiltrate Indian Kashmir territory, incite the locals to revolt, and provide them with arms and assistance for this purpose.[46] In the second stage, with the region already in a state of disorder, regular Pakistani troops would cross over. Bands of guerrillas started crossing into Indian Jammu and Kashmir from training camps in Azad Kashmir in early 1965. However, instead of welcoming them the local population reacted either with indifference or hostility.[47] Aware by late August 1965, of Pakistani intensions, the Indians launched a counter move aimed at blocking off further entry from Azad Kashmir. Indian troops crossed the ceasefire line on 24th August and occupied certain passes in the Tithwal region.[48] The Pakistan army entered in the Chambh district of Jammu, aiming to cut the Pathankot road from Jammu to Srinagar—the main line of communication for the Indian forces. Their advance was quite successful; by Fifth September they were within 20 miles of Jammu. But at this point they received their second shock.

On Sixth September, with Jammu in danger of falling, India launched a counter offensive across the international Indo-Pak border, towards Lahore. On Eighth September, Indian troops crossed the Indo-Pak border in the far south, aiming for Karachi. With these offences Kashmir conflict escalated into a full-scale war between India and Pakistan. Neither side was successful in achieving its military objectives. The Indians managed to hold onto Jammu and the vital Pathankot road. The Pakistanis managed to save their major cities—Lahore, Sailkot and Karachi—from falling to the enemy. A stalemate was reached on all fronts. With little to gain from protracted hostilities, and with virtually the entire international community urging cessation, both sides agreed to an UN-mediated ceasefire.[49] This took effect on 23th September, 1965. The 1965 war strained the economies of both the countries. It was devastating for Pakistani unity because it revealed to the East Wing that Pakistan was a Punjab-centric state whose army defined both the idea of Pakistan and the security parameters of the state of Pakistan in a manner that was incompatible with Bengali interests. When Ayub Khan (President of Pakistan) stated that the defence of Pakistan lay in the West, he effectively wrote off East Pakistan.[50] After the war, the USSR took the initiative and convened a meeting of the heads of the two states at Tashkent.

Tashkent Declaration—1966

By 1965, Russia had changed its Khrushchev era attitude of being strongly pro-Indian on the issue of Jammu and Kashmir, to a more neutral stance under the leadership of Alexei Kosygin.[51] Even before hostilities had started, on August 1965, Kosygin had offered to act as mediator on negotiations between India and Pakistan. At that time both the parties had rejected this offer. However, when it was repeated on 17th September with Tashkent suggested as a possible meeting place, Shastri accepted almost immediately, and Ayub Khan some months later (on 25th November). Talks between Kosygin, Shastri and Ayub Khan were scheduled to start in Tashkent on Third January 1966. Initially and indeed until virtually the last moment, there was little hope of the talks generating any kind of agreement as the two parties positions were simply too far apart. However, both India and Pakistan realised that failure in Tashkent could result in renewed hostilities, with unpredictable consequences. Hence, on 10th January, they did sign an agreement, the Tashkent Declaration. This was less an agreement ending the Kashmir dispute, as one allowing it to be pushed to one side so that the two countries could resume relatively normal relations. Its main point was that both sides forces would withdraw to the positions they had held before hostilities began. (dated 5th August).

Other practical points included repatriation of prisoners-of-war and resumption of diplomatic relations. More generally, the Declaration committed both sides to 'settle their disputes through peaceful means,' and 'to non-interference in the internal affairs of each other,' and to 'promote the development of friendly relations between the two countries'. Finally, it was agreed that the bilateral talks would be continued.[52] The Tashkent Declaration did not deal with the Kashmir dispute other than to note its existence. In effect, it suggested that the issue should be put into cold storage while other more urgent problems were being solved.[53] Prisoners-of-war were repatriated and by 25 February, 1966 the forces of India and Pakistan had withdrawn to their pre-fifth August positions.

Significance for Politics within Jammu and Kashmir

The period of Indo-Pak relations up to the signing of the Tashkent Declaration was to prove immensely significant for political developments within Jammu and Kashmir. There was a decline of external interest in the State. The UN had by 1958 reached a stalemate in its efforts to resolve the situation and had effectively left it to India and Pakistan to settle through bilateral negotiations. Meanwhile, Pakistan, which had since 1947 persistently taken a keen interest in Kashmiri affairs, also appeared to bow out after 1965. The Pakistanis had made a military grab for the State and failed; the Kashmiri people themselves had given them a poor reception; and increasingly Pakistani leaders were distracted by internal power struggles. All these considerations led Pakistan to accept (practically if not formally) the stalemate there.[54] When external pressure considerably lessened, New Delhi felt far more confident about further integrating Jammu and Kashmir with rest of India. The decline in external interest also forced political elites within the State, notably Sheikh Abdullah, to strive for the best possible deal within India. The other aspect of this period that was to be significant for future political developments within the State were the UN resolutions stipulating the Kashmiris 'right to self-determination'.[55]

Indo-Pak War—1971

After the signing of Tashkent Declaration very little attempt was made by either side to permanently resolve the problem of Jammu and Kashmir. On 30th January, 1971, an Indian Airline plane (the 'Ganga') flying from Srinagar to Jammu was hijacked by two Kashmiris and forced to land in Lahore. Claiming to be Kashmiri freedom fighters, the hijackers demanded India to release some thirty six prisoners belonging to a group called the Kashmir National Liberation Front.[56] The hostages were returned to India the next day, but the hijackers destroyed the aeroplane before Pakistan could comply with the Indian demand that it too be handed back. In view of the Pakistani hesitation in returning the plane, their refusal to return the hijackers over to the Indian police and the general support in Pakistan for the hijacking, India accused the Pakistani Government of assisting the hijackers. On 4th February, it banned the over flight of all Pakistani aircraft (civil and military) across Indian Territory.[57] Ayub Khan had been overthrown in a military coup in March 1969. His successor, Yahya Khan, had promised to hold free elections to install a civilian government. The elections were originally scheduled for October but were held in mid-December. The results of the National Assembly elections as well as the East Pakistan Provincial Assembly Poll produced a landslide victory for Sheikh Mujibur Rahman's Awami League. The party won 162 out of the total of 313 seats in the National Assembly, securing a clear majority. Similarly, his party won 288 out of 300 seats in the Provincial Assembly.[58] However, the West Pakistan establishment and even more so Zulfikar Ali Bhutto (leader of the Pakistan People's Party which won the most votes in West Pakistan) were unwilling to be ruled by a Bengali government. Predictably, the failure to hand over power to the Awami League led to the widespread public protests in East Pakistan. Yahya Khan responded to these protests with a military crackdown, leading in turn to armed resistance by the Bengali Mukti Bahini, a force partly trained and armed by India.[59] As more and more Bengali refugees fled across the border to India, New Delhi sent its forces into East Pakistan to openly assist the Mukti Bahini. Pakistan responded by invading India from the West on 3rd December, 1971, and later launched attacks into Indian Jammu and Kashmir. The Indians countered by attacking West Pakistan in Sindh and north Punjab, and by also crossing the cease-fire line in Jammu and Kashmir. The war did not go well for Pakistan, especially in the eastern wing were it faced strong local opposition as well as supply and communications problems (increased by the Indian over flight ban). On 17th December, Pakistani forces in Dhaka surrendered unconditionally to Indian forces, ending the third Indo-Pak war after just fourteen days. Although this Indo-Pak war had been fought largely outside Jammu and Kashmir, its consequences—aside from the obvious emergence of Bangladesh—were critically felt in that State.[60]

Simla Agreement—1972

The Simla Agreement of 1972 was another attempt to normalise Indo-Pak relations after war. While the 1971 war had ostensibly been over Bengali separation, Bangladesh-once-created was not an obstacle to friendly Indo-Pak relations. The status of independent Bangladesh was soon recognised by the international community, and even within Pakistan pragmatic elements felt that the loss of the East wing was a blessing in disguise; it would certainly make future nation building much easier.[61] The real obstacle to harmony in the subcontinent was still Jammu and Kashmir; and thus it was primarily this issue that was addressed in the Simla Agreement. However, like the 1966 Tashkent Declaration, the Simla Agreement did not attempt to permanently resolve the dispute over the status of Jammu and Kashmir. It took the easier option of putting this 'on hold' so that progress could be made in other aspects of the two countries dealing. Between 28th June and 3rd July, 1972, after talks at lower levels had been held since April, and following a great deal of international diplomacy by both sides, Zulfikar Ali Bhutto and Indira Gandhi met in Simla to try to restore some order to Indo-Pak relations.[62] The two sides went to the negotiating table with very different objectives. India wanted the cease-fire line to become the *de facto* international boundary. It was not particularly interested in gaining control of the entire state. In addition, despite having initiated UN involvement in Jammu and Kashmir, it now wanted all external bodies excluded and future negotiations to be on a strictly bilateral basis. Pakistan, in contrast, persisted with its claim to the entire State and was not prepared to accept the cease-fire line as a permanent boundary. It also opposed ending UN involvement in attempts to resolve the dispute. Coupled with these differences was the desire by both not to be perceived domestically as having 'lost face'.[63]

In 1966, Ayub Khan and Lal Bahadur Shastri had gone to Tashkent as 'equals'. The 1965 war had ended in a stalemate so there was no clear 'winner' and 'loser'. But in 1972, Bhutto and Mrs Gandhi were definitely meeting as 'vanquished' and 'victor'. In addition, India held nearly 94,000 Pakistani prisoners of war, and some 5000 square miles of territory in what was formerly West Pakistan.[64] Despite all this Mrs Gandhi went to Simla in a conciliatory mood, aware of Bhutto's need to placate domestic public option, and the agreement which was signed appeared to favour neither side's position. The main points of the Simla Agreement were:

(i) Both sides would settle future problems through bilateral negotiations or 'any other peaceful means';

(ii) Both sides would respect the cease-fire line, referred to as the line of control; neither would unilaterally seek to alter it;

(iii) The UN Charter would govern relations between the two countries;

(iv) Representatives of the two sides would meet to discuss normalisation of relations including a final settlement of Jammu and Kashmir.[65]

Close examination of the terms of this agreement reveals it to actually be much closer to the Pakistani than the Indian position. The inclusion of 'any other peaceful means' certainly did not exclude future UN involvement in Jammu and Kashmir, a point reaffirmed in the reference to the UN Charter. 'Line of Control' was not synonymous with international boundary, while the phrase 'future settlement of Jammu and Kashmir' implied Indian Sovereignty in the State was far from acknowledged as permanent.[66] Following the signing of the Simla Agreement, the general Indian view was that Jammu and Kashmir was now a permanent part of the Indian Union, and that the threat to this position from Pakistan had largely disappeared. This thinking, especially in central government circles, profoundly influenced policies towards the State.[67]

Significance for Politics within Jammu and Kashmir

The 1971 Indo-Pak War and the subsequent Simla Agreement affected the Kashmir politics in the same way as the 1965 war and Tashkent Declaration, six years earlier. As far as Pakistani policy-making was concerned Kashmir was very much pushed onto the backburner. The 1971 defeat in war had shown the Pakistanis that Kashmir could not be won by force from India, and the chances of internal rebellion handing the State to them appeared remote. In terms of political developments, Sheikh Abdullah and the National Conference were forced to deal with India. The prime issue became not whether accession was final or not, but what the status of Jammu and Kashmir would be within India. Political freedom within the State was largely restored: about 160 political prisoners, including Maulana Masoodi, were released shortly after the 1971 elections. In April, Begum Abdullah was allowed to return to Kashmir and in June the internment order against Sheikh Abdullah was lifted, quickly followed by those against Beg and G. M. Shah. Sheikh Abdullah returned to Srinagar on 19th June, 1972. The ban on the Plebiscite Front was not lifted, but neither was it renewed when it expired on 12th January, 1973.[68]

The Indian Nuclear Explosion—1974

Perhaps the most important development of the earlier half of the seventies was the Indian nuclear explosion. India exploded a nuclear device code-named 'Smiling Buddha' on 18th May 1974. Although India stressed that it was a Peaceful Nuclear Explosive (PNE), the difference between explosions for peaceful and military purposes was viewed as indistinguishable. Pakistan's response to the Indian explosion was a mixture of frustration and aspiration. Reacting to India's explosion, the Pakistani Prime Minister Bhutto again stressed that the people of Pakistan would never accept Indian hegemony or succumbs to its nuclear blackmail. While there is no doubt that Bhutto had repeatedly expressed the need to acquire nuclear capability even prior to becoming the president of Pakistan, the two main determinants of Pakistan's quest for nuclear capability were the dismemberment of Pakistan in 1971 and the Indian nuclear explosion of 1974.

Kashmir Accord—1975

Since the internment order against Sheikh Abdullah was lifted, he was allowed to return to Srinagar on 19th June, 1972. Initially he lost no time in declaring that the people of the Jammu and Kashmir still enjoyed the right to self-determination. On hearing of the Simla Agreement of 2nd July, 1972 he pointed out that neither India nor Pakistan were entitled to decide the fate of the State of Jammu and Kashmir over the heads of its people.[69] However, by the end of 1973, some shift in his position became apparent. He condemned Bhutto for meddling in the internal affairs of Jammu and Kashmir and indicated a willingness to enter into negotiations with the Indian Government on the State's status within India. What prompted this shift can only be speculated at but one possible explanation is that having been out of power for almost twenty years, Sheikh Abdullah was eager to grasp at the last chance (in view of his age) to recapture it. Besides, the division of Pakistan had its own impact on the course of events inside the state of Jammu and Kashmir. The extent of the subsequent compromise made by Abdullah to New Delhi suggests retaining the premiership was the major motivating factor.[70]

Negotiations between the Indian Government and leaders of the Plebiscite Front began early in 1974. There were high profile meetings between Indira Gandhi and Abdullah, but most of the detailed negotiations took place between Mirza Afzal Beg and Mrs Gandhi's special representative, G. Parthasarathi. These two had come up with an agreement by November 1973, which was approved by Abdullah on 12th February, and made public by Indira Gandhi on 24 February, 1975. It was known as the Kashmir Accord.[71] In the Accord, Sheikh Abdullah did not achieve his ambition for a return to the exact position as it had been prior to his dismissal in August 1953. From Sheikh Abdullah's point of view, the major compromise was acknowledgement of the finality of Jammu and Kashmir's accession to India. Article 370 was retained, thereby supposedly allowing the state a high degree of autonomy within the Indian Union. However, closer examination of the Accord revealed Article 370 to be very much in name only, all the post-1953 changes reducing Kashmiri autonomy such as Article 356 (allowing Centre to assume power) were retained. Indian parliament will continue to make laws relating to the prevention of activities directed towards disclaiming, questioning or disrupting the sovereignty and territorial integrity of India. The terms Prime Minister and Sadar-i-Riyasat-potent symbols of autonomy were not to be brought back.[72] The publication of the Accord was accompanied by prompt political action. On 23rd February, 1975, Syed Mir Qasim resigned as Chief Minister of the State of Jammu and Kashmir. Two days later the congress party in the State Legislature, which controlled it, unanimously elected Sheikh Abdullah its leader and Mirza Afzal Beg as a Cabinet Minister. On 4th March, in New Delhi the Accord received the approval of the Lok Sabha by a massive majority and the Rajya Sabha agreed to it on 13th March, 1975.[73] The Kashmir Accord, even during the negotiation stage, attracted some vocal opposition in the Vale of Kashmir. In the first half of 1974, Mirwaiz Farooq accused Abdullah of 'selling out' to India.[74] In Jammu and New Delhi, Jana Sangh supporters demonstrated violently against the Accord and argued that the Article 370 of the Indian Constitution be abrogated and the whole of the State of Jammu and Kashmir incorporated into the Indian Union just like any other State. In Pakistan also the Accord was denounced as a "sell-out". Z. A. Bhutto had particularly strong words for Sheikh Abdullah's perfidy when he observed that this man who had set himself up as the champion of democracy was now about to become

Head of a Government dominated by a party, Congress, to which he did not belong, in an Assembly of which he was not even a member.[75] There was an impressive *hartal* throughout Pakistan on 28th February, 1975 and overseas Pakistanis and Kashmiris in the United Kingdom and elsewhere held demonstrations. On 1st March, 1975, Pakistan protested to the United Nations and argued that the Accord violated both the 1972 Simla Agreement and the United Nations requirements for a Kashmir plebiscite. These were gestures only and had the Accord happened in earlier times, the result could well have been the prelude to another Indo-Pak armed conflict.[76]

Siachen Clashes—1984

The Siachen Glacier is one of the most inhospitable and glaciated regions in the world. Sliding down a valley in the Karakoram Range, the glacier is 76 kilometers long and varies in width between two to eight kilometers. It receives up to six to seven meters of the annual total of 10 meters of snow in the winter months. Blizzards can reach speeds of up to 150 knots (nearly 300 kilometers per hour). The temperature drops routinely to 40 degrees centigrade below zero, and even lower with the wind chill factor. For these reasons, the Siachen Glacier has been called the 'Third Pole.'[77] The UN ceasefire line was physically demarcated in accordance with the 1949 Karachi Agreement, up to the edge of the glacier region. From the Siachen to the Karakoram pass, recognised international practice was applied. It was decided to demarcate this glacier area at some later stage. The status quo was not disturbed even during the Indo-Pak wars of 1965 and 1971.[78] Geopolitical compulsions of India, Pakistan and China brought it to the centre stage because it was part of a region where the three nations attempted to impose their military control. The military compulsions led to the militarising of the Siachen area more than the mountaineering needs of either India or Pakistan.[79] New Delhi first became suspicious in 1983 when an American map showed the Siachen and places like Lyogme and Lagongma as part of Pakistan. Subsequently, the Indian army came to know that a Japanese mountaineering expedition team was seeking Islamabad's permission to scale certain mountains in the area.[80] India launched *Operation Meghdoot* on 13th April, 1984, when the Indian Army and the IAF went into the glacier.[81] Pakistan quickly responded with troop deployments and what followed was literally a race to the top. Within a few days, the Indians were in control of most of the area, as Pakistan was beaten to most of the Saltoro Ridge high ground in about a week. In 1987, Pakistan made an attempt to dislodge the Indian positions. The unsuccessful attack was carried out under the command of Gen. Pervez Musharraf, and the positions remained the same.[82] Over the years Indian expedition proved disastrous.[83] India eventually agreed to negotiate and the two sides managed to reach an agreement after the conclusion of the fifth round of talks. The agreement was announced on 17th June 1989, but this agreement was never implemented because the Indian leadership got apprehensive of the likely reaction in India and decided to put it in cold storage, where it is still languishing.[84]

Exercise Brasstacks—1986

Another crisis that emerged in the second half of the eighties was the product of the Indian military exercise called 'Brasstacks' which started towards the end of 1986. The Indian military leadership stressed that the exercise was meant to test new concepts and introduce mechanisation. Since the exercise was conducted close to the Pakistani borders, the Pakistanis initially saw it as a form of intimidation and later began to sense the danger of a likely Indian invasion. The Pakistanis responded by stationing their troops at strategic places close to the Indian border. Thus, the atmosphere became loaded with tension, which influenced the two countries to initiate diplomatic negotiations. The negotiations were soon able to secure the desired accord and the crisis was successfully defused.[85]

Insurgency in Kashmir—1989

While the post-1947 political history of Indian Kashmir was at times turbulent and a separate ethno-national consciousness remained consistently strong among Kashmiri Muslims, it was only in the late 1980s that widespread frustration among Kashmiri Muslims against some of their own leaders and the policies pursued by New Delhi erupted into a full-blown secessionist movement.[86] The administrative and civil administration was brought down by two sets of forces: the secessionist groups headed by the (relatively) secular Jammu and Kashmir Liberation

Front (JKLF) demanding independence and union of the Indian and Pakistan sides of Kashmir and the irredentist groups headed by the Islamic Hizbul Mujahedeen seeking unification with Pakistan.[87] The catalytic event had been the 1987 elections when the newly formed but unpopular coalition between the Indian Congress party and the state's ruling National Conference party rigged the assembly elections and deprived the dissident groups of representation in the new legislature. Then, during 1988, several separatist leaders crossed the border to the Pakistan controlled Azad Kashmir, received training and weapons and returned to the Valley prepared for political insurgency.[88] The leader of JKLF Yasin Malik has said that they took arms in 1989 when they found that people could not get power through the ballot box.[89] Coinciding with the outbreak of separatism in Kashmir, India and Pakistan embarked on a proxy war that did not involve any actual military to military combat in a conventional sense after a formal declaration of war. It involved three different types of conflict: diplomatic confrontation to win international support, aiding and abetting of the insurgency by Pakistan, and India's counterinsurgency response and the periodic exchange of fire by Indian and Pakistani forces across the LoC in Kashmir. In the midst of the Kashmir Muslim insurgency, tensions between India and Pakistan became so intense that in May 1990, the Pakistani military headed by General Mirza Aslam Beg was willing to use nuclear weapons to 'take out New Delhi.' It was President George H. W. Bush's National Security Advisor Robert Gates and Assistant Secretary for Middle Eastern and South Asian Affairs who reportedly helped arrest a deadly encounter between them by visiting India and Pakistan.[90]

Male Spirit—1997

A month before the Male summit was held, the foreign ministers of India and Pakistan met and discussed all outstanding issues. The meeting was hailed as congenial and part of an ice-breaking process.[91] In the same month, Indian foreign minister, I. K. Gujral became the prime minister of India. In May 1997, in Male, the capital of the Maldives, on the sidelines of a South Asian Association for Regional Cooperation (SAARC) summit, Indian Prime Minister Inder Kumar Gujral and his Pakistani counterpart Nawaz Sharif mooted the idea of a structured dialogue or the Composite

Dialogue Process (CDP).[92] I. K. Gujral, a visionary and thinker (also known for his 'Gujral Doctrine' which called for a constructive and pro-active relationship with South Asian neighbours on a non-reciprocal basis) and Nawaz Sharif, whose government was in absolute majority in the National Assembly provided the necessary political will that was required for the realisation of such an initiative. Based on a compromise approach, the peace process enabled the two countries to discuss all issues including Jammu and Kashmir, simultaneously. In other words, the peace process discarded the 'Kashmir first' approach and followed a middle-path wherein progress on all issues was possible simultaneously. It was a compromise in the sense that while India agreed to include Kashmir in the agenda for talks, Pakistan relented to include terrorism, the two major irritants in bilateral relations.[93]

Nuclear Explosions of May—1998

Atal Bihari Vajpayee while addressing the Indian Parliament after China carried out nuclear tests in 1964 declared: 'the answer to an atom bomb is an atom bomb, nothing else.'[94] On 11 and 13th May 1998, the BJP government in India stunned the world by conducting a series of nuclear tests. India's reasons to opt for weaponisation were many. While Indian defence minister referred to the Chinese threat as the major influencing factor, the Indian Prime Minister Vajpayee's letter to the then US President Clinton revealed that India's decision to go ahead with the nuclear tests was due to the deteriorating security environment.[95] Vajpayee goes on to mention the war with China in 1962 and the three aggressions we have suffered in the last fifty years from Pakistan and for the last ten years we have been the victim of unremitting terrorism and militancy sponsored by it especially in Jammu and Kashmir.[96] On 28th May, Pakistan conducted its own nuclear tests. The Indian acquisition of nuclear weapons radically altered the security scenario in the region. Pakistani security managers impressed upon the decision makers to remedy the situation. With the incumbent gap in conventional arms, the push towards nuclearisation following the Indian nuclear accomplishments is somewhat understandable. The most important factor that influenced Pakistan's decision to opt for nuclear weapons was the Indian threats on Kashmir.[97] Following Advani's tough talk regarding Kashmir after the nuclear tests, a fear psychosis gripped the Pakistanis that India was actually planning to attack Pakistan. The Pakistanis also argued that they had credible information that India was planning to attack Pakistan's nuclear installations.[98]

Bus Diplomacy and the Lahore Declaration

The earliest months of 1999 saw a major positive development which seemed to have revived the Male Sprit, at least for a short while. On 20th February, Indian Prime Minister Vajpayee rode a bus into Pakistan along with a group of eminent Indians for a two day visit. He was warmly and enthusiastically received at the border by his counterpart in Pakistan, Nawaz Sharif. Stepping out of the bus on Pakistani soil the Indian prime minister described his visit as the 'defining moment in the South Asian history'.[99] While the two prime ministers could hardly afford to ignore the negative baggage of the past 52 years, they made efforts to put the relationship on the right track. The two day visit produced the 'Lahore Declaration', along with a Memorandum of Understanding and a joint statement. Both countries agreed to take immediate steps to reduce the risk of a nuclear conflict between them, sincerely negotiate with each other to resolve all outstanding issues including the Kashmir dispute, introduce more CBM's (Confidence Building Measures) like agreeing to provide advance notification of ballistic missile tests, and also periodically review the implementation of existing CBMs, and reiterated their determination to implement the Simla Agreement in letter and spirit, hold consultations to further liberalise visa restrictions, review the communication links, engage in bilateral consultation on security, disarmament and non-proliferation issues, conclude an agreement in order to prevent incidents at sea, and to ensure the safety of naval vessels, aircrafts belonging to the two sides, etc.[100] The Lahore declaration has opened up many avenues for cooperation and amity. But if the atmosphere built by Vajpayee's visit and Nawaz Sharif's generous approach is allowed to be dissipated, events will meander to the same old situation. Even if there is no conflict, there will be no settlement, even if no hostility, no harmony and, even if there is no war, there will be no peace. Both countries would have missed the bus.[101]

Kargil Affair—1999

Three months after the historic visit of Vajpayee, fighting flared up on the LoC, particularly Kargil area. The Kargil crisis had its antecedents in an ongoing dispute over the location of the LOC as it passes through the Siachen glacier, one of the highest and most inhospitable heights in the Himalayas. Kargil is situated on Highway 1-A from Srinagar to Leh, which is the only land route to supply Indian troops on the glacier.[102] Controlling the high ground over Kargil would allow Pakistan to cut off the Indian supply route. Sporadic low level hostilities began in 1984 and continued into the late 1990's. Beginning in the fall of 1998, Pakistani light infantry troops, accompanied by mujahidin volunteers, infiltrated undetected across the LoC to establish positions on the Himalayan peaks, which Indian troops regularly abandoned during the harsh winter months. When returning Indian troops discovered the Pakistani emplacements the following May, the ensuing fighting led to "a short, sharp, war."[103] India's attempts to dislodge the Pakistani troops led to high casualties and little success until Indian air strikes, coupled with strong American diplomatic pressures, led to a Pakistani withdrawal. The Kargil episode presents us with a number of puzzles. One among them is the *timing* of the Pakistan's military operation. It occurred just a few months after a summit meeting between Nawaz Sharif and Vajpayee at Lahore which had led to a relaxation in tensions. A Second puzzle surrounds the operation's objective-what its organisers expected to gain by it. Was it a payback operation replying to India's seizure of the Siachen Glacier in April, 1984? [104]

The report of the Kargil Review Committee commissioned by the Indian government to investigate multiple aspects of the Kargil episode, identify eight suggested motivations for Pakistan's undertaking of the Kargil intrusions. They classify them as follows:

Political-Strategic Motives

1. To internationalise Kashmir as a nuclear flashpoint requiring urgent third party intervention;
2. To alter the Line of Control (LoC) and disrupt its sanctity by capturing unheld areas in Kargil; and

3. To achieve a better bargaining position for a possible trade-off against the positions held by India in Siachen.

Military/Proxy War-Related Motives

4. To interdict the Srinagar-Leh road by disrupting vital supplies to Leh;
5. To outflank India's defences from the South in the Turtok and Chalunka sectors through unheld areas, thus rendering its defences untenable in Turtok and Siachen;
6. To give a fillip to militancy in Jammu and Kashmir by military action designated to weaken the counter insurgency (CI) grid by drawing away troops from the Valley to Kargil. It would also give a boost to the morale of militants in the Valley;
7. To activate militancy in the Kargil and Turtok sectors and open new routes of infiltration into the Valley; and
8. To play to the fundamentalist lobby and the Pakistani people by bold action in Kashmir, which continues to remain a highly emotional issue.[105]

Kargil intensified the deep Indian distrust of Pakistan, which Indian leaders now characterised, in the jargon of the day, as a "rogue state." India's Prime Minister Vajpayee, who expended a good deal of political capital on the Lahore summit, complained that he had been "stabbed in the back".[106] The Kargil experience could not help but only reinforced the Indian view that the only way to deal with Pakistan was through the application of force, a perspective reflected in the Kargil Review Committee Report.[107] When the fighting concluded, India announced plans to create a new army corps headquarters in Kashmir (14th Corps, at Leh in Ladakh) as well as to station one of its mountain divisions permanently in the Kargil sector, steps whose financial requirements were bound to be substantial.[108]

Agra Summit—2001

The Kargil episode taking place against the backdrop of the region's move to overt nuclear weaponisation had heightened the urgency of revived official dialogue between India and Pakistan. It had made the most emphatic case possible for a more resolute regional commitment to Kashmir's settlement.[109] It took almost one year after the fighting ended at Kargil before the first major sign surfaced of any softening in the formal positions of either side on Kashmir. It came on 24th July 2000 in the form of a unilateral declaration of a three-month ceasefire by Hizbul-Mujahideen, one of the most powerful as well as the most indigenously rooted of the Kashmiri militant organisations. The cease-fire appeared to have Islamabad's at least tacit approval.[110] It was greeted enthusiastically by New Delhi, which quickly ordered its own security forces to observe a cease-fire while at the same time initiating talks with the Hizbul-Mujahideen commanders. A second and still more momentous sign of possible movement toward more conciliatory government (Indian and Pakistani) postures on Kashmir came about four months later, on 19th November, when Indian Prime Minister Vajpayee announced that Indian security forces in Jammu and Kashmir would observe a month-long unilateral cease-fire of their own.[111] This one was to commence on 28th November with the onset of the Islamic holy month of Ramadan.[112]

On 23rd May, 2001 Indian government abruptly terminated the cease-fire, by then in its sixth month, coupled with a seemingly incongruous invitation to General Pervez Musharraf, viewed in India as the architect of Kargil, to visit India.[113] Fifty-two days later, on 14th July, the Pakistani President arrived in India for talks. [114] The talks were held at Agra, known as the site of the Mughal architectural gem, the Taj Mahal. The Agra Summit failed ignominiously. The documents support the President Musharraf and his foreign minister's version. The draft Agra Declaration did no more than set up a new mechanism for resolution of pending issues. It's first Article provided that "settlement of the Jammu and Kashmir issue would pave the way for normalisation of relations between the two countries."[115] Foreign ministers Jaswant Singh and Abdul Sattar revised it jointly in their own hands. Initially the Indian modification read "progress on addressing outstanding issues, including Jammu and Kashmir and the establishment of a cooperative relationship will be mutually reinforcing." Abdul Sattar proposed a further modification which both wrote out to read thus: "progress towards settlement of Jammu and Kashmir would be conducive towards normalisation and will further the establishment of a cooperative relationship in a mutually reinforcing manner." Jaswant Singh took this agreed draft back and promised to return in 15 minutes. He did not. Instead as hours passed Pakistan's High Commissioner Ashraf Jehangir Qazi was informed that the talks were off.[116]

Thus the Agra Summit ended abruptly late in the evening of 16th July, 2001 without agreement having been reached on the wording of a declaration or joint statement, without a press conference, and, indeed, without even a photographed final handshake. On Kashmir, neither side was willing to stray too far from long-standing maximalist official formulations—India's that Kashmir had to be linked with cross-border terrorism; Pakistan's that Kashmir was primarily a problem of human rights and self-determination.[117]

Notes

1. Stephen Philip Cohen, *The Idea of Pakistan*, Oxford University Press, New Delhi, 2004, p. 5.
2. T.V. Paul, *The India-Pakistan Conflict: An Enduring Rivalry,* Foundation Books, New Delhi, 2006, p. 6.
3. Stanley Wolpert, *A New History of India*, Oxford University Press, 2000, p. 317.
4. Stephen Cohen, *op. cit.*, p. 6.
5. T.V. Paul, op. cit. p. 7.
6. *Ibid.*
7. Iffat Malik, *Kashmir: Ethnic Conflict, International Dispute*, Oxford University Press, 2005, p. 21.
8. "Of Nehru and Edwina", *The Hindu,* July 20, 2007.
9. T.V. Paul, op. cit., p. 8.
10. Sumantra Bose, *Kashmir: Roots of Conflict, Paths to Peace*, Vistaar Publications, New Delhi, 2003, pp. 165, 168.
11. *Ibid.,* pp. 168-70.
12. T.V. Paul, *op. cit.*, p. 9.
13. If implemented, the central government in Delhi will limit its jurisdiction in Kashmir to defence, foreign affairs, communications,

and currency while the authority of the India Election Commission and Supreme Court will still be maintained over the state. Harish Khare, "Kashmir: New Roadmap Taking Shape," http://www.hinduonnet.com, November 18, 2004.

14. In November 2004, Indian Prime Minister Manmohan Singh reiterated the inviolability of India's territorial boundaries, but hinted at the possible Indian cessation of loose borders between the two Kashmirs and considerable autonomy for the Kashmiri population. Dr Singh was responding to Pakistan President Pervez Musharraf who had proposed the creation of seven demilitarised autonomous regions on both sides of Kashmir, granting some of them independence or giving the option of joint control by India and Pakistan or placing them under UN mandate. "Indian PM Rejects Kashmir Proposal," *BBC News,* November 17, 2004.
15. S.S. Bindra, *Indo-Pak Relations: Tashkent to Simla Agreement*, Deep and Deep Publications, New Delhi, 1981, p. 24.
16. UNMOGIP Background, http://www.un.org/en/peacekeeping/missions/unmogip/background.shtml.
17. K.R. Gupta, *India-Pakistan Relations with Special Reference to Kashmir*, Atlantic Publishers and Distributors, New Delhi, 2003, p. 887.
18. S.S. Bindra, *op. cit.*, p. 24.
19. Sisir Gupta, *Kashmir: A Study in India-Pakistan* Relations, Asia Publishing House, Bombay, 1966, pp. 220-221.
20. S.S. Bindra, *op. cit.,* p. 24.
21. *Ibid.*
22. *Ibid.*
23. Iffat Malik, *op. cit.*, p. 98.
24. *Ibid.*
25. Ajit Bhattacharjea, *Kashmir: The Wounded Valley*, UBSPD, New Delhi, 1994, p. 189.
26. *Ibid.*
27. Iffat Malik, *op. cit.*, p. 99.

28. *Ibid.* p. 102.
29. M.J. Akbar, *Kashmir: Behind the Vale*, Viking Penguin, New Delhi, 1991, pp. 142-143.
30. Iffat Malik, *op. cit.*, p. 103.
31. *Ibid.*
32. S.M. Burke, *Mainsprings of Indian and Pakistani Foreign Policies*, Minneapolis: University of Minnesota Press, 1974, p. 143.
33. S.S. Bindra, *op. cit.*, p. 26.
34. S.R. Bakshi, *Kashmir through Ages*, Volume-5, Sarup and Sons, New Delhi, 1996, p. 111.
35. The Henry L. Stimson Center, "*The Indus Waters Treaty", Stimson,* <http://www.stimson.org/southasia/?sn=sa20020116300>
36. *Ibid.*
37. Seema Sridhar, "*Kashmir and Water: Conflict and Cooperation*", *Programme in Arms Control, Disarmament, and International Security* (ACDIS), University of Illinois at Urbana-Champaign, 2008.
38. *Ibid.*
39. *Ibid.*
40. S.S. Bindra, *op. cit.*, p. 34.
41. *Ibid.*
42. W.M. Dobell, "*Ramifications of the China-Pakistan Border Treaty*", Pacific Affairs, Vol. 37, No. 3 (Autumn, 1964), pp. 287-288.
43. *Ibid.*
44. Alastair Lamb, *Kashmir: A Disputed Legacy 1846-1990*, Oxford University Press, Pakistan, 1991, p. 256.
45. *Ibid.*
46. Iffat Malik, *op. cit.*, p. 122.
47. *Ibid.*
48. *Ibid.*
49. Alastair Lamb, *op.cit.*, p. 265.
50. Stephen Cohen, *op. cit.*, p. 73.

51. Iffat Malik, *op. cit.*, p. 123.
52. *Ibid.*
53. Alastair Lamb, *op. cit.*, p. 271.
54. *Ibid.*
55. *Ibid.*
56. Alastair Lamb, *op. cit.*, p. 288.
57. *Ibid.*
58. J.N. Dixit, *India-Pakistan in War and Peace*, Ashok Chopra, Book Today, New Delhi, 2002, p. 170.
59. Iffat Malik, *op. cit.*, p. 137.
60. *Ibid.*
61. Alastair Lamb, *op. cit.*, p. 296.
62. *Ibid.*
63. Iffat Malik, *op. cit.*, p. 139.
64. A Govt. of Pakistan White Paper, published later in 1977, cited in Alastair Lamb, *Kashmir: A Disputed Legacy 1846-1990,* p. 296.
65. Iffat Malik, *op. cit.*, p. 140.
66. *Ibid.*
67. *Ibid.*
68. *Ibid.*, p. 141.
69. Alastair Lamb, *op. cit.*, p. 304.
70. Iffat Malik, *op. cit.*, p. 143.
71. *Ibid.*
72. *Ibid.,* p. 144.
73. Alastair Lamb, *op. cit.*, p. 308.
74. *Ibid.*
75. *Ibid.*
76. *Ibid.*
77. Samina Ahmad and Varun Sahni, "*Freezing the Fighting: Military Disengagement on Siachen Glacie*r", Cooperative Monitoring Center Occasional Papers (Sandia National Laboratories, Albuquerque) 1998, pp. 9-10.

78. P.R. Chari and Pervaiz Iqbal Cheema, *The Simla Agreement 1972: Its Wasted Promise*, Manohar Publishers, New Delhi, 2001, p. 168.
79. Lt. Gen. V.R. Raghavan, *Siachen: Conflict without End*, Viking Penguin Books, New Delhi, 2002, p. 29.
80. Kuldip Nayar, *Wall at Wagah: India-Pakistan Relations*, Gyan Publishing House, New Delhi, 2003, p. 232.
81. Rajesh Kumar, *Getting to Rapprochement Over Kashmir: Is Using the 'China Model' a Viable Alternative*, RCSS, Colombo, Sir Lanka, 2007, p. 20.
82. *Ibid.*
83. Ayesha Siddiqa-Agha, *Pakistan's Arms Procurement and Military Build-up, 1979-99: In search of a policy*, Palgrave, 2001, p. 20.
84. P.R. Chari and Pervaiz Iqbal Cheema, *op. cit.*, p. 164.
85. *Ibid.* p. 168.
86. Rajat Ganguly, "India, Pakistan and the Kashmir insurgency: causes, dynamics and prospects for resolution", *Asian Studies Review,* Routledge, UK, 2001, p. 310.
87. *Ibid.*
88. *Ibid.*
89. Kuldip Nayar, *op. cit.*, p. 241.
90. Seymour Hersh, "*On the Nuclear Edge*," The New Yorker, March 29, 1993.
91. *Dawn,* 10 April 1997.
92. Ashutosh Misra, "*An audit of the India-Pakistan peace process*", Australian Journal of International Affairs, Vol. 61, No. 4, Routledge, UK, 2007, p. 507.
93. *Ibid.*
94. Kalpana Sharma, "*The Hindu Bomb*", The Bulletin of the Atomic Scientists, Chicago, USA, July 1998, p. 30.
95. Arundhati Roy, "*The End of Imagination*", The Guardian, UK, August 1, 1998.
96. *Ibid.*
97. P.R. Chari and Pervaiz Iqbal Cheema, *op. cit.*, 175.
98. *Ibid.*

99. Amit Baruah, "*The Bus to Pakistan*", Front line, India, March 12, 1999.
100. *The News,* 22 February 1999.
101. Kuldip Nayar, *op. cit.*, p. 213.
102. T.V. Paul, *op. cit.*, p. 114.
103. *Ibid.*
104. Robert G. Wirsing, *Kashmir in the Shadow of War: Regional Rivalries in a Nuclear Age,* Spring Books Gurgaon, India, 2004, p. 38.
105. *Ibid.*, p. 43.
106. Harjinder Sidju, "*Ansari Arrest Proves Pak Hand*: PM," *Hindustan Times,* Feb. 11, 2002.
107. The Kargil Review Committee Report, 1999.
108. Robert G. Wirsing, *op. cit.*, p. 58.
109. *Ibid.*
110. *Ibid.*
111. At its inception, the Indian cease-fire was formally described as "*non-initiation of combat operations*" (NICO).
112. Pamela Constable, "*Indian Announces One-Month Cease-fire in Kashmir; Unilateral Move at Opening Talks With Rebel Groups,*" Washington Post, 20 November 2000, p. 11.
113. Robert G. Wirsing, *op. cit.*, p. 61.
114. *Ibid.*
115. A.G. Noorani, "India-Pakistan Peace Process", *Institute of Regional Studies,* Seminar Papers, Islamabad, 20-21 Oct. 2008, pp. 135-136.
116. *Ibid.*
117. Atul Aneja, "Reconstructing the Agra Summit," *The Hindu*, 27 July 2001.

2

Issues and Components in the Composite Dialogue Process

India and Pakistan have a long history of conflicts and wars since 1947. Although they resolved the Indus Waters dispute in 1960 and the Rann of Kutch dispute in 1968 through negotiations, there was no agreed mechanism to navigate their enduring conflictual relationship. In the 1980s the two sides began to confer on the Siachen, Sir Creek and the Tulbul-Wullar disputes and put in place a series of confidence building measures pertaining to conventional and nuclear weapons power.[1] These negotiations had no set time table and were held on need to meet basis.

It was in May 1997, at Male, the capital of Maldives, the then Indian Prime Minister Inder Kumar Gujral and his Pakistani counterpart Nawaz Sharif mooted the idea of a structured dialogue or the Composite Dialogue Process (CDP). [2] The dialogue process is composite being focused on making progress simultaneously on all the major issues of bilateral dispute. The Foreign Secretary level meeting of June 23, 1997 agreed to constitute Joint Working Groups (JWGs) on eight issues that were identified to be discussed between India and Pakistan.[3] Based on a compromise approach, the peace process enabled the two countries to discuss all issues including Jammu and Kashmir, simultaneously. It was a compromise in the sense that while India agreed to include Kashmir in the agenda for talks, Pakistan relented to include terrorism, the two major irritants in bilateral relations.[4] The Lahore Agreement of February 1999 had reiterated the desire of the two countries to move forward on the path of dialogue. The Kargil War in June-July 1999, the failed Agra Summit in July 2001, the attack on India's Parliament on December 13, 2001 and the subsequent mobilisation of troops on the border led to the difficult phase in the bilateral relations. This phase saw active US and British mediatory efforts whose significance cannot be under-estimated. A joint statement issued on 27th March 2003, after a Bush-Blair summit at Camp David laid down a detailed road map which both India and Pakistan followed. It bears recalling: "The United States and the United Kingdom condemn all terrorism wherever it occurs and whatever its purported justification, we will continue to work with our partners to eliminate this scourge, violence will not solve Kashmir's problems. Pending the resolution of these problems, the LoC should be strictly respected and Pakistan should fulfill its commitments to stop infiltration across it. Pakistan should also do its utmost to discourage any acts of violence by militants in Kashmir. Both sides should consider immediately implementing a ceasefire and taking other active steps to reduce tension including by moves within the SAARC context. The differences between India and Pakistan can only be resolved through peaceful means and engagement."[5]

After a gap of more than two years, both the countries agreed to revive the process of Composite Dialogue in February 2004.[6] This became possible only after the President of Pakistan General Pervez Musharraf assured Prime Minister Vajpayee that he would not allow any part of the territory under Pakistan's control to be used to support terrorism against India.[7, 8] In a significant move, troops along the border disengaged following the cease-fire along the LoC, International Border (IB) and the Actual Ground Position Line (AGPL) in November 2003.[9] The 12th SAARC summit of 2004 saw a change in the history of this conflict. Specific suggestions were made by the PM of Pakistan Zafarullah Jamali in the context of India-Pakistan relations to resume civil aviation links, road and rail links, sports events etc.[10] Subsequently, the foreign secretaries of the two countries met on February 18, 2004, to start the process of Composite Dialogue. The Composite Dialogue Process (CDP) deals with the following eight issues:

(i) Peace and Security including CBMs
(ii) Jammu and Kashmir

(iii) Siachen
(iv) Wullar Barrage Project/Tulbul Navigation Project
(v) Sir Creek
(vi) Terrorism and Drug Trafficking
(vii) Economic and Commercial Cooperation and,
(viii) Promotion of Friendly Exchanges in various fields[11]

Each round of dialogue is initiated and reviewed by the foreign secretaries; the overall progress is reviewed at the Ministerial level. So far four rounds of Composite Dialogue have been completed. The fourth one was started in March 2007 and completed in August 2007. Apart from dialogue on the eight issues provided above, technical and expert level talks on Nuclear CBMs, Conventional CBMs, Cross Line of Control CBMs, Cooperation between Coast Guards, Narcotics Control Agencies, Civil Aviation, etc., are also being held regularly.[12]

1. Peace and Security including CBMs

The term CBM covers a very large canvas ranging from a simple unwritten understanding between the two adversaries to a treaty.[13] A journey from simple understanding to the signing of a treaty could be viewed as a part of the CBM process provided confidence is generated between the adversaries at various stages of progression. A CBM is a bilateral or a multilateral measure that builds confidence, arrests the undesirable drift towards open hostilities, reduces tensions, and encourages the adversaries to make contact for negotiations without taxing too much the operative policy pursuits.[14] There is no doubt that more and more CBMs could further improve atmosphere for talks but one should also realise that CBMs do not solve conflicts; they merely make the atmosphere conducive for talks. If the talks keep extending or injecting more and more CBMs but has nothing to show on the conflict resolution front, then disappointment begin to pile up which could result in impeding the effective implementations of already agreed CBMs.[15]

In the backdrop of nuclear tests conducted by India and Pakistan in May 1998, the two traditional regional rivals and their neighbours in South Asia and beyond are now stakeholders in any efforts that would reduce tensions, build confidence and encourage regional cooperation. The political and economic stability of the countries of the region, individually and collectively, are dependent on the ability of the region to develop sustainable, achievable and effective set and process of CBMs and institutionalised regional co-operation.[16] The injection of CBMs is not really a new phenomenon in South Asia in general and between India and Pakistan in particular. Since the hurried departure of the British from South Asia and the partition of the Indian subcontinent, both India and Pakistan have signed many agreements aimed to generate confidence and reduce tensions. Among them perhaps the most notable are; Liaquat–Nehru Pact (1950), Indus Water Treaty (1960), Tashkent Agreement (1966), Rann of Kutch Agreement (1968), Shimla Accord (1972), Salal Dam Agreement (1978), and the establishment of the Joint Commission (1983).[17]

With the exception of the Joint Commission, all others were the products of either a crisis or a war that necessitated a logical end to the preceding developments.[18]

The main conflict between India and Pakistan revolves around the Kashmir dispute. Despite the advent of so many CBMs, the normalisation still seems somewhat of an elusive pursuit.[19]

Since the end of the 1971, Indo Pak war, many CBMs have been adopted with a pronounced emphasis upon military CBMs initially. The earliest one came immediately after the 1971 war. A 'Hotline' between the DGMOs (Directors General of Military Operations) was established in 1971.[20]

The existing CBMs can be grouped broadly into four categories; communication, notification, consultation, and goodwill measures. Communication Measures includes measures like DGMOs hotline, hotline between sector commanders, hotline between two air forces, naval vassals, Prime Ministers hotlines, people to people contacts, track II diplomacy, NGOs, dialogue between non-governmental groups like Neemrana Initiative etc.[21]

Similarly, notification measures include advance notification regarding military exercises or missile tests. Inviting other side's military observers to military exercises or making joint declaration such as prohibition of chemical weapons etc., are deemed as good CBMs. The consultation measures include measures like joint India-Pakistan Commission or Foreign Secretary level talks. The goodwill measures include participation of various officials, both civilian and military, to various seminars and conferences, exchange of sports teams to play matches in each other's country, visits of non-official and officials, and regular official meetings etc.[22]

The Composite Dialogue Process was reviewed in 2004. The past record indicates that the network of CBMs has been gradually expanding and the atmosphere has vastly improved for negotiations. The negotiation itself may or may not result in the resolution of conflicts. The CBMs must be viewed as means and not an end itself. A review of the past couple of decades clearly reveal that the introduction of the CBMs have alleviated the situation and reduced tensions. A close scrutiny of crises like the Brasstacks (1987), Crisis of 1990, Kargil clashes (1999) and troop's confrontation (2002) clearly recognise the varied contributions made by the CBMs. The most recent manifestation of CBMs contributions is the vastly improved atmosphere that has enormously facilitated the resumption of communication and transportation links and has also vastly increased opportunities for people to people contacts. While the usefulness of CBMs cannot be more CBMs, it is also recognised by almost all concerned that the time has come to show some tangible results on the conflict resolution front. Both Siachen and Sir Creek disputes are ripe for resolutions and their resolution is bound to strengthen the ongoing peace process and could also facilitate enormously the negotiations over a complex dispute like the ongoing Kashmir dispute.[23]

2. Jammu and Kashmir

A cursory look at the events in the last decade would reveal that India, Pakistan and even Kashmiris have reached the Mutually Hurting Stalemate (MHS) stage on Kashmir, and that there is no way other than reaching an understanding at the political level. It is clear, that none of the parties involved in the conflict—India, Pakistan, Kashmiris and militants, can alter the status quo through military means. The status quo, on the other hand is also not acceptable, as it is hurting all the parties concerned.[24]

India and Pakistan have failed to alter the status quo in Kashmir, irrespective of the different political and military strategies that they employed in recent years. Before the Islamabad Summit in January 2004, there have been more than thirty-five occasions, in which the Heads of State in India and Pakistan met on various occasions. Besides these meetings at the highest levels, there were at least twelve rounds of talks between 1989 and 1998 before the Lahore and Agra Summits. Neither the meetings at the Heads of State level nor at the Foreign Secretary level, could proceed further. All these attempts invariably broke down, due to the failure of both governments to reach an understanding on Kashmir. The dialogue at the Secretary level in 1998 and that of the Lahore process in 1999, in particular were crucial, as both of them took place in the post-nuclear tests period. The 1998 talks at the Secretary level began with a lot of promise; the joint statement issued by the Foreign Secretaries of India and Pakistan in September 1998 read:[25]

> At each round the Foreign Secretaries will hold separate meetings on (a) peace and security including CBMs and (b) Jammu and Kashmir and review the progress of the dialogue process. The Foreign Secretaries will commence the substantive dialogue with separate meetings on (a) peace and security including CBMs and (b) Jammu and Kashmir in Islamabad on 15-18 October, 1998. The remaining six subjects i.e., (c) Siachen, (d) Wullar Barrage/Tulbul Navigation Project, (e) Sir Creek, (f) Terrorism and Drug Trafficking, (g) Economic and Commercial Cooperation, and (h) Promotion of friendly exchanges in various fields, shall be taken up in substantive and separate meetings in New Delhi in the first half of November 1998.

Despite the failure of the talks at the Foreign Secretary level, the Prime Ministers of India and Pakistan in 1999 made yet another attempt to reach an understanding on all issues including Jammu and Kashmir. According to the Lahore declaration, both India and Pakistan:[26]

- Shall intensify their efforts to resolve all issues, including the issue of Jammu and Kashmir.
- Shall refrain from intervention and interference in each other's internal affairs.

- Shall intensify their composite and integrated dialogue process for an early and positive outcome of the agreed bilateral agenda.
- Shall take immediate steps for reducing the risk of accidental or unauthorised use of nuclear weapons and discuss concepts and doctrines with a view to elaborating measures for confidence building in the nuclear and conventional fields, aimed at prevention of conflict.
- Reaffirm their commitment to the goals and objectives of SAARC and to concert their efforts towards the realisation of the SAARC vision for the year 2000 and beyond with a view to promoting the welfare of the people of South Asia and to improve their quality of life through accelerated economic growth, social progress and cultural development.
- Reaffirm their condemnation of terrorism in all its forms and manifestations and their determination to combat this menace.
- Shall promote and protect all human rights and fundamental freedoms.

Besides the open diplomacy between the two countries, unknown to the outside world, including their foreign offices, the two Prime Ministers were also engaged in secret negotiations through their trusted emissaries. There were at least six rounds of talks between R. K. Mishra and Niaz Naik, who were widely believed to be the emissaries of Vajpayee and Nawaz Sharif respectively, before the conflict in Kargil shattered the calm. The first round between R. K. Mishra and Anwar Zahid, the younger brother of Akram Zaki—a distinguished Pakistani diplomat, took place during Third and Fourth March 1999 in Islamabad. Niaz Naik replaced Zahid, after the latter's untimely death due to severe illness. Naik and Mishra met in Islamabad on 20th March, 1999. The third round of talks between the two took place in New Delhi between 27 March and 1st April, 1999. The fourth, fifth and sixth rounds took place in Islamabad on 12th April, 21st April and 17th May in Islamabad.[27] Unfortunately, none of these processes could be sustained over a period, so that a peace process could be firmly established towards the final resolution of the bilateral conflicts, especially that of Kashmir. Besides the political approach, both governments intermittently also attempted a military approach to alter the status quo in Jammu and Kashmir. The Kargil conflict, theories of limited war and preemptive strikes and the border confrontation in 2002—all were reflections of the attempt to alter the status quo in Jammu and Kashmir, militarily.[28] Following the Kargil conflict, there was a serious attempt from a section in the Indian strategic community to alter the status quo in India's favour through a limited war or pre-emptive strikes. The main belief from the Indian side was that a limited war could be fought with Pakistan under the nuclear umbrella. George Fernandes, the then Indian Defence Minister, one of the pioneers of limited war with Pakistan stated that nuclear weapons, "can deter only the use of nuclear weapons, but not all and any war" and under the nuclear shadow, a "conventional war remained feasible though with definite limitations if escalation across the nuclear threshold was to be avoided."[29] The 2002, border confrontation, though its immediate cause was a terrorist attack on the Indian Parliament on 13th December, 2001, had an underlying assumption that India could wage a limited war with Pakistan, so as to prevent the latter from supporting the separatist movement in the Indian Kashmir. The military build-up started after the 13th December, 2001 attack on the Indian Parliament. New Delhi blamed Jaish-e-Muhammad, Lashkar-e-Taiba and Pakistan; while Islamabad categorically denied any involvement in the attack and offered a joint investigation. The Indian Prime Minister announced on December 2001, that the attack on Parliament was an attack on 'the very existence and honour' of the nation and warned that all options were open.[30] Using the military build-up, a section inside India wanted to bargain hard with Pakistan. According to them India failed to convert the military victory in 1971 into a political victory, by resolving the Kashmir conflict once and forever.[31] Whatever the initial efforts, India realised later that war was not an option. War with Pakistan would not bring economic, political and strategic dividends. If the Kargil confrontation could not alter the status quo for Pakistan, the border confrontation of 2002 could not do the same for India. Clearly, there is no military option, either for India or for Pakistan.

In 2001 and 2002, India undertook two major initiatives towards Kashmir. First was an internal ceasefire, followed by the appointment of K. C. Pant and latter N. N. Vohra as the government's chief interlocutors. The 2002 elections witnessed the Peoples Democratic Party (PDP) led by Mufti Mohammad Sayeed forming the coalition government along with the Congress and other parties. The elections were relatively fair and free, as compared to the earlier ones. In April 2003, there was a breakthrough, when Vajpayee offered 'hand of friendship' speaking from Srinagar.[32] Ultimately, in October 2003, India proposed twelve confidence building measures, including the resumption and extension of air and rail link, a new bus service between Srinagar and Muzaffarabad, liberalisation of the visa regime, and permitting people over sixty-five years of age to cross the border at Wagah on foot.[33] Islamabad reciprocated with its own set of CBMs. Islamabad offered to start an additional bus service from Lahore to Amritsar, revival of rail links, a hundred scholarships for Kashmiri students, free treatment of forty Indian patients in Pakistani hospitals, and a proposal for rehabilitation of Kashmir victims, etc.[34]

3. Siachen

The highest battlefield in the world, the Siachen Glacier, has witnessed conflict between India and Pakistan for over twenty years. It has so far resulted in hundreds of causalities caused mostly by adverse climatic conditions and harsh terrain rather than military skirmishes. The conflict is also putting an enormous financial burden on the national exchequer of both sides. Sliding down a valley in the Karakoram Range, the glacier is 76 kilometers long and varies in width between two to eight kilometers.[35] It receives up to six to seven meters of the annual total of 10 meters of snow in the winter months. Blizzards can reach speeds of up to 150 knots (nearly 300 kilometers per hour). The temperature drops routinely to 40 degrees centigrade below zero, and even lower with the wind chill factor. For these reasons the Siachen Glacier has been called the "Third Pole."[36] The altitude of some Indian forward bases on the Saltoro Ridge range from Kumar (16,000 feet) and Bila Top (18,600 feet) to Pahalwan (20,000 feet) and Indira Col (22,000 feet). Because of the steep gradient of the Saltoro Range, the area is also prone to avalanches. Only three per cent of the Indian causalities have been caused by hostile firing and the remaining 97 per cent fall prey to the altitude, weather, and terrain.[37] Pakistani positions are comparatively at a lower altitude in the glacier area, ranging between 9,000–15,000 feet. Initially, Siachen was considered to be completely inhospitable and not worth any conflict on the ground. The original cease fire line (CFL) agreed to by India and Pakistan in the July 1949, Karachi Agreement did not cover the area of 'the glaciers' because of the difficulties of delineating the line. Beyond the delineated grid, Point NJ 9842, near Chalunka, the Karachi Agreement spoke of the line passing 'north to the glaciers'.[38] When the ceasefire line was changed into a mutually accepted line of control (LoC) in October 1972, the newly delineated line ran from the Shyokriver west of Thang (which is in India) to Point NJ 9842. The area north of it was left blank and open to encroachments. Indians and Pakistanis have tried to stake their territorial claims by interpreting the vague language contained in the 1949 and 1972 agreements to prove their respective points. For Pakistan 'thence northwards' means from NJ 9842 up to Karakoram Pass.[39] India, on the other hand draws a north westerly line from NJ 9842 along the watershed line of the Saltoro Range, a southern offshoot of the Karakoram Range.[40]

The genesis of the Siachen dispute was the April 1984 Indian military initiative in the vicinity of the Siachen Glacier. The operation, code-named *Meghdoot*, triggered armed clashes between Indian and Pakistani forces in the area and eventually led to the current phase of dispute.[41] Continuous negotiations have been held to contain and resolve the conflict ever since the outbreak of hostilities. As early as 1984 and 1985, flag meetings were held with a little success between Indian and Pakistani sector commanders. Since January 1986, several high-level talks have been held between Indian and Pakistani defense and foreign secretaries as well as senior military personnel, reflecting their desire to reach a peaceful and negotiated settlement. In 1989 and once again in 1992, the two countries came close to a resolution of the dispute.[42] At the fifth round of talks between Defence Secretaries in June 1989, an understanding was initially reached to resolve the dispute. According to the joint statement issued at the conclusion of talks, "there was agreement by both sides to work towards a comprehensive settlement, based on redeployment of forces to reduce the chances of conflict, avoidance of the use of force and the determination of future positions on the ground so as to conform with the Simla Agreement and to ensure durable peace in the Siachen area." The joint statement stated that, "The army authorities of both sides will determine these positions.[43]" At the sixth round of the Defence Secretary talks in November 1992, with the assistance of military experts, an India-Pakistan agreement was reportedly reached that envisaged; (1) the mutual withdrawal of troops from key passes to new positions, and (2) the creation of a 'zone of complete disengagement' as a result of troop disengagement and redeployment. The delineation of this area of 'peace and tranquility' would be "without prejudice" to the known position of either side. The agreement also

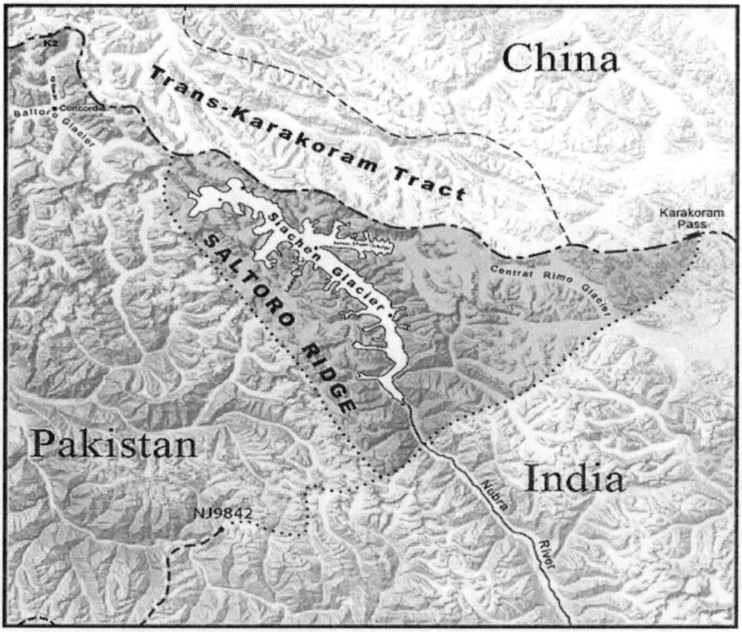

Map 2. Siachen Glacier and the Surrounding Areas

Under the Karachi agreement the border extended to a point known as NJ9842 'and thence north to the glaciers'.

Map courtesy: http://www.flickr.com/photos/amapple/2561626234

reportedly included pledges by both states to refrain from reoccupying vacated positions.[44] No new positions would be occupied in the designated zone nor would any activity-civilian or military be allowed within the designated zone. Time schedules for disengagement and redeployment were to be worked out to the 'mutual satisfaction' of both sides, followed by the formation of a joint commission that would be responsible for 'delineation of the Line of Control beyond NJ 9842.' Until the area was formally delineated, monitoring mechanisms would be devised to prevent the occurrence of violations.[45] The two countries, however, not only failed to implement these tentative agreements, but one or the other side denied that any tangible agreement had been reached on either occasion.[46] The difficulty in reaching or implementing any mutually agreeable proposal was due to a number of factors, ranging from domestic political constraints to differences over the determination of redeployment positions, the demarcation of the proposed demilitarised zone, and ensuring the inviolability of such a zone. The significance of the understandings reached in 1989 and 1992 cannot, however, be understated since they identify potential areas of agreement and discord in any future agreement of the Siachen dispute.

4. Tulbul Navigation Project/ Wullar Barrage

India and Pakistan disagree even on the name of this dispute. India refers to it as Tulbul Navigation Project (TNP) whereas Pakistan calls it the Wullar Barrage.[47] The TNP originally envisaged the construction of 439-feet long and 40-feet wide barrage by India in 1984 on the River Jhelum, at the mouth of Wullar Lake, near Sopore town in Kashmir. With a maximum storage capacity of 0.30 million acre feet (MAF), it was intended to maximise the utilisation of water at India's largest fresh water lake, making the Jhelum navigable by regulating water storage in the Wullar through enhancing currents in the Jhelum during the lean months from November to February. The dispute arose when Pakistan alleged that this barrage would critically hinder the flow to Pakistan. It was considered by them to be a violation of the Indus Waters Treaty of 1960. India rebuffed these allegations and stated that the primary reason for building the barrage was to make the river navigable in the summer months.[48] Since the dispute was linked to the Indus Water Treaty, it was brought up for discussion between the Indus Water Commissioners of India and Pakistan in May 1986. During these discussions, India argued that the Barrage could be built on Wullar Lake for navigational purposes. Islamabad feared that under the cover of a 'navigational project', India wanted to control Jhelum's water and subsequently use it for the generation of hydro-electric power. In December 1987, the Commissioners met again for further discussions. In these talks, India argued that since Wullar Lake was not a part of the river Jhelum, India had every right to construct a 'dam' or 'barrage' on it. In reply, Pakistan wrote to New Delhi on 2nd January, 1988, saying that the Jhelum Main starts from Verinag. As clearly stated in the 1960 Treaty, all tributaries join each other in Wullar Lake and the river

Jhelum flows from the lake. Therefore, building a dam on the Jhelum Main would constitute a violation of the Treaty.[49] In the meantime Pakistan also sought the advice of a committee of British and American experts on the subject, who suggested that Muhammad Khan Junejo, the then Prime Minister, should approach the International Court of Justice. However, Junejo did not implement the report of the committee. On the other side, in a significant move, India abandoned the construction work until any agreement was reached, through direct talks and discussions.

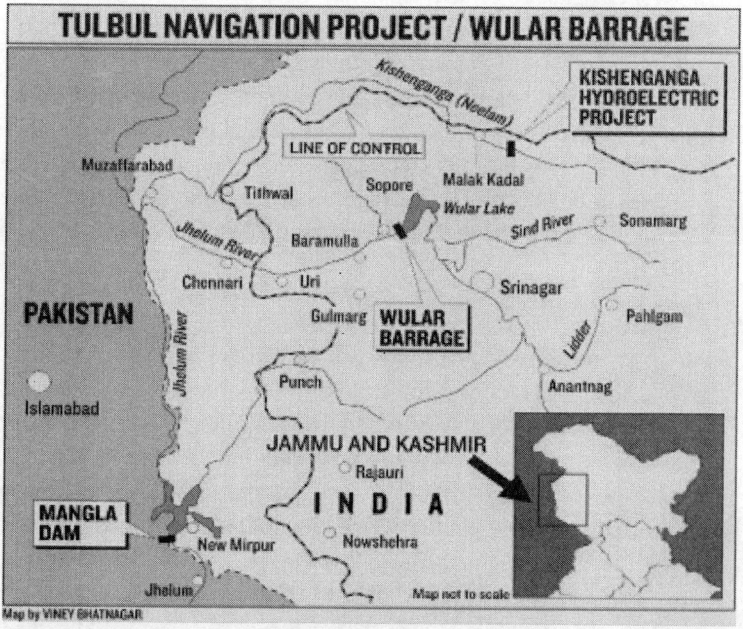

From 1987 to 1992, eight rounds of Secretary level talks were held between Indian and Pakistan. The basic draft agreement on the dispute had been arrived at in October 1991.[50] Initially, the barrage was to be gated. After Pakistan's objections, it was decided to un-gate it. This is reflected in the stipulations of the 1991 draft agreement. In the agreement the two sides agreed that: (a) India would keep 6.2 meters of the barrage un-gated with a crest level at EL 1574.90 metres; (b) India would not make any alteration in the salient features of the project without mutual agreement between the two countries; (c) India shall forego the general storage capacity of 30,000 acre feet out of the provision permitted to it on the

Jhelum (excluding Jhelum Main); (d) in return for this, the water level in the barrage will be allowed to attain the full operational level of 5177.90 feet– the timing of the filling of the lake will be decided by the two Indus Water Commissioners and, should they fail to reach an agreement, the filling of the lake would be between June 21 and August 20; (e) except for the stipulation regarding the filling of the lake, India would let all the waters entering the Wullar Lake downstream; and (f) all differences will be settled under the provisions of the Indus Water Treaty.[51] Later, in addition to the above, Pakistan demanded that India forego the construction of the 390 MW Kishenganga hydroelectric project. Its argument was that this project would affect Pakistan's proposed Neelum-Jhelum power project. New Delhi did not give any such commitment. The 1991 draft was reproduced verbatim in the non-papers handed over to Pakistan by India in 1994. During the 1998 composite dialogue process, the Pakistani delegation had apparently insisted on starting the talks afresh whereas India insisted that the threads should be picked up from the 1991 draft.[52]

5. Sir Creek

The India-Pakistan dispute over Sir Creek can be traced back to the pre-independence period, to around 1908, when an argument ensued between the rulers of Kutch and Sind over a pile of firewood lying on the banks of a creek dividing the two principalities. The dispute was taken up by the government of Bombay state, which, in 1914, gave its verdict supported by Map Number B44 and subsequently B74.[53] Nothing significant happened in the next 40-50 years, and the dispute again came alive only in the 1960s. Sir Creek, which is more like a fluctuating tidal channel, is a sixty-mile-long estuary in the marshes of the Rann of Kutch. The Rann lies on the border between the Indian state of Gujarat and the Pakistani province of Sind. In 1965, after armed clashes, Pakistan asserted that half of the Rann along 24th parallel was Pakistani territory. India countered that the boundary ran roughly along the northern edge of the Rann. The matter was referred to arbitration and the Indo-Pakistani Western Boundary Case Tribunal's Award on February 19, 1968, upheld 90 per cent of India's claim to the entire Rann, conceding small sectors to Pakistan.[54] This still left the boundary of the Sir Creek from its head in the marshy lands of the Rann to its mouth in the Arabian Sea and the maritime boundary between India and Pakistan un-demarcated. India and Pakistan had agreed not to refer this part of the un-demarcated boundary for adjudication to the tribunal. Because of this understanding between the parties, the tribunal had noted that it had not taken into consideration the boundary along the Sir Creek.[55] The dispute has festered since then. As a result, it is not possible for India and Pakistan to distinguish between their territorial waters (the zone up to 12 nautical miles, where states enjoy exclusive rights and can restrict passage of foreign boats), their contiguous zones (up to 24 nautical miles, where states can enforce custom and fiscal laws, fisheries laws and ban acts prejudicial to the state) or their Exclusive Economic Zones (up to 200 nautical miles extendable to 350 nautical miles for countries with continental shelf).[56]

Pakistan's contention is that the boundary along the Sir Creek must lie along the eastern edge of the creek. India believes that the boundary should be along the middle of the creek; that it should be demarcated using the 'thalweg' or the mid-channel principle ('thal'-valley, 'weg'-way). The 'thalweg' principle lays down that boundaries along a river or a valley must lie along the line connecting the deepest points along a river channel or the lowest points along the valley floor. The case for a mid-channel boundary is based on the Sir Creek being a navigable channel throughout the year. Pakistan's contention is that the creek is not navigable and, therefore, the mid-channel principle does not apply. Today, the Sir Creek does not flow as shown in the 1914 map. It has shifted westwards i.e., towards Pakistan. However, the head of the creek, as it existed then, is marked by a boundary pillar, called Western Terminal. It was from this point that some 38 pillars marked the horizontal boundary eastwards. Pakistan neither recognises the existence of the Western Terminal nor the pillar-based horizontal boundary eastwards. Pakistan's contention is that the eastward boundary should be based on the dotted line as drawn in the 1914 map. This line is below the boundary marked by the pillars. The contentious question is: What should be recognised – the pillars on the ground or the line on the 1914 map? In the current climate, neither country is willing to concede territory.[57]

So, the dispute remains where it was. Pakistan is insisting on the left bank of the creek and the dotted line on the 1914 map as the boundary and India insisting on the mid-channel of the creek and the pillars to the east as the boundary. Several rounds of talks were held between the two countries to resolve the dispute.

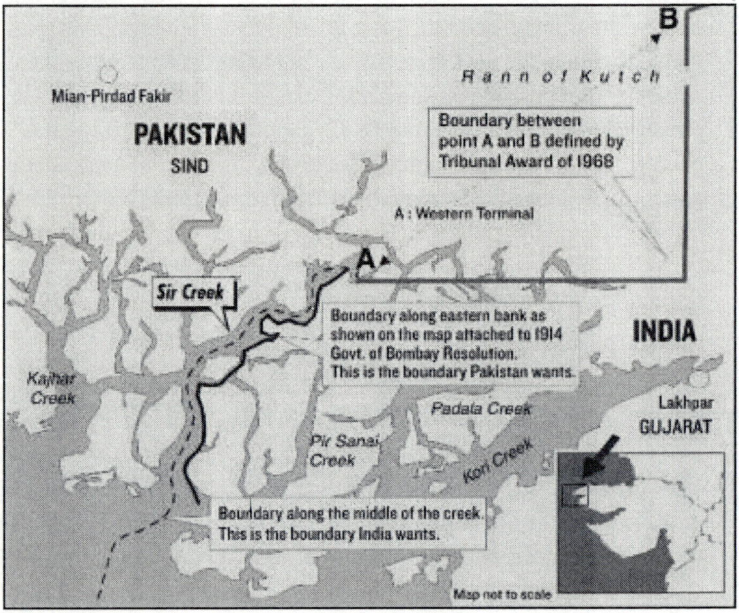

Map 4. Sir Creek Disputed Areas.

During the first round of talks held in Islamabad on Second June, 1989, the Indian and Pakistani delegations were led by the Surveyor-General, Major General S.M. Chadha and the Surveyor-General, Major General Anis Ali Syed respectively. At these talks, the two sides only managed to discuss the fundamental aspects of the dispute, but no concrete results eventuated. Later, several rounds of talks were held from 1990 to 1992 without making any substantial progress.[58]

6. Terrorism and Drug Trafficking

One of the driving factors for India to agree to a composite dialogue was to address the issue of terrorism. The 2001-2002 India-Pakistan military stand-off took place against the backdrop of war on terror in the region. The attack on the Jammu and Kashmir state assembly in Srinagar on October 1, 2001 and subsequent attack on the Indian Parliament on December 13, 2001 precipitated a 10-month military stand-off between the two countries. Pakistan for the first time condemned the attack on the state assembly and the Indian Parliament.[59] The thaw in India-Pakistan relations began in April 2003 and resulted in ceasefire on the LoC on 26th November, 2003.[60]

The joint statement that formed the basis of Indo-Pak composite dialogue hinged on drawing a delicate balance between India's concern on terrorism and Pakistan's apprehension regarding the marginalisation of the Kashmir issue. The statement said: "the resumption of the composite dialogue will lead to peaceful settlement of all bilateral issues, including Jammu and Kashmir". Islamabad agreed that it "would not permit any territory under Pakistan's control to be used to support terrorism in any manner."[61] The issue of terrorism is acting as a stumbling block to the Indo-Pak peace initiatives. The origins of state-sponsored terrorism in Pakistan could be traced to the Soviet military intervention in Afghanistan in 1979 and the consequent involvement of Pakistan as a frontline state supporting the Mujahedeen groups in the Afghan civil war.[62]

One of the major offshoots of Pakistan's involvement in the Afghan war and its subsequent support to the Taliban regime in Afghanistan (1996–2001) was the growing impact of the role of drugs in Pakistan. Along with Iran and Afghanistan, Pakistan has become a part of the Golden Triangle notorious for poppy cultivation and illegal traffic in drugs. As the production of all the intoxicants was declared illegal in Iran after the revolution, the heroin laboratories from Iran were shifted to Pakistani Baluchistan in the early 1980s.[63] Over the years, the impact of drugs and drug-related activities has permeated every major walk of contemporary Pakistan. With the Iranian blockade under the revolutionary regime, the Indo-Pakistan border became vulnerable to transactions in arms and drugs. The drug barons in Pakistan rooted these items through the states of Punjab, Rajasthan and Gujarat.[64] The situation has worsened for India since the reports of the International Narcotics Control Bureau reveal that the quantity of heroin entering India from Pakistan has increased, with the law and order agencies in northwestern India seizing ever increasing consignments that are being smuggled from Pakistan and Afghanistan. However, of greater concern is the finding in the report that, from being the final destination, India is becoming a transit point for drug trafficking to Bangladesh and Southeast Asia.[65]

7. Economic and Commercial Cooperation

Trade cooperation between India and Pakistan was a direct outcome of the partition of Indian sub-continent on August 14, 1947. At that time, India and Pakistan were highly dependent on each other for trade. Thereafter, both resorted to deliberate measures to minimise their trade dependence on each other. India's share in Pakistan's global exports and imports was 23.6 per cent and 50.6 per cent, respectively in 1948-49. These shares went down to 1.3 per cent and 0.06 per cent in 1975-76, and 1.1 per cent and 2.7 per cent, respectively in 2005-06.[66] Similarly, Pakistan's share in India's global exports and imports was 2.2 per cent and 1.1 per cent, respectively, in 1951-52. These shares went down to 0.02 per cent and 0.4 per cent in 1975-76, and 0.7 per cent and 0.13 per cent in 2005-06.[67] This shows that the trade between these two neighbouring countries has been much below the potential. In fact, the period between 1965 and 1971 witnessed two wars between India and Pakistan. Immediately after the war, Pakistan imposed official embargo on her trade with India. The trade relations between the two neighbouring countries remained suspended for nine years and created problems for both the countries. The resumption of trade relations between them took place with the signing of bilateral trade agreement on January 23, 1975.[68] But the flow of trade was restricted to government levels. This trade agreement expired on January 22, 1978 and thereafter trade has continued without any agreement. In July 1982, Pakistan declared a list of 40 items in which private sectors of the two countries could trade. The mutual trade has grown significantly since 1989, when Pakistan expanded the list of approved imports from India to 571 items, and further enhanced it to 600 items on July 17, 2000, and 1075 items on November 3, 2006.[69]

There are opposing views on the significance of enhanced bilateral trade between the two countries. One view holds that trade between the two countries would facilitate cheaper access to goods for the consumers in both the countries. While others believe that India being the larger economy tends to dominate the economic interactions between the two countries. The existing trade between India and Pakistan is conducted via three different ways: official trade which is dismal and non-official trade and illegal trade. Since the bilateral trade is marred by multiple issues, the official trade between the two countries has not been able to cross the limited volume. India also associates the official trade with granting New Delhi of MFN status (most favour favoured nation status) by Pakistan. India granted Pakistan MFN status in 1995 but Pakistan still is reluctant to reciprocate. Though this act of Pakistan is viewed as a violation of the SAFTA, the country maintains its reluctance. Nonofficial trade, on the other hand, has grown, as there are certain items which are not on the positive list of the two countries. These items are traded via third country such as United Arab Emirates, especially Dubai.[70] The informal trade is estimated at some two billion to three billion dollars per annum. Moreover, there are a number of goods that are traded illegally across the border which only serves the vested interests of the illegal traders.

Potential sectors for economic cooperation between the two countries include agricultural products, especially tea, auto spare-parts, minerals, chemicals, pharmaceuticals, leather, textiles, telecommunications, iron ore, energy resources, electricity generation using coal and wind energy. Of all the above-mentioned sectors, there is an immense scope for cooperation in energy sector and textiles, especially ready-made traditional garments.[71] There is also a large scope of trade in private service sectors such as health, entertainment services, information technology, and tourism. India and Pakistan have mostly common multinational companies operating in their respective countries for instance, Standard Chartered, Unilever and Glaxo Smith Kline (GSK), which are a force to be harnessed as they can act as meaningful conduits for trade and investment if they source raw material from each other.[71] The SAFTA also provides an opportunity to India and Pakistan to gear up intra-regional multilateral trade which is bound to open up newer avenues not only for the two countries but also for their regional neighbours.

There are several key reasons why trade between India and Pakistan needs to be enhanced. First, viewed in a larger regional context, South Asia is the least integrated region and stronger economic relations between India and Pakistan is key element of regional integration in South Asia. Second, there are vast untapped trade and investment possibilities between the two countries which can be gainfully exploited with significant welfare gains for their populations. Third, as natural trading partners with a common border, trading with each other can be substantially higher as the potential is estimated to be 10 times the current level.[72]

The major constraint in Indo-Pak trade is the mindset of the people on both sides of the border. A section in Pakistan feels that a softening of the border would lead to India dumping goods in Pakistan, which would hurt the local Pakistani traders. In India, the biggest concern against expanded trade relations is security.[73] Another major irritant in bilateral relations has been the continued use of a *"positive list"* by Pakistan in its trade with India. SAFTA expects its members to cut tariffs to between zero and five per cent within seven years of the start of the agreement.[74] All the member countries, except Pakistan, have implemented SAFTA in full, which still trades on the basis of a positive list. Pakistan, on the other hand, claims that India's non-tariff barriers act as a greater obstacle to trade relations.[75]

8. Promotion of Friendly Exchanges in Various Fields

Talks under the Friendly Exchanges include arts and culture, education, Ayurvedic and Unani medicine, archaeology, tourism, youth affairs, sports and media. Over the years, exchanges such as cricket matches, visits by academicians, professionals, peace activists and journalists constructively contributed to building mutual understanding and friendship. Cricket has helped in bridging the divide, allowing the fans from both sides to travel to the other country to watch the match and enjoy mutual hospitality. Such exchanges have shaped peoples' perceptions positively in both countries towards each other.

In 1987, General Zia-ulHaq flew to Jaipur, in India, to witness a match. General Musharraf followed suit almost two decades later, coming to watch an India-Pakistan match in New Delhi during his state visit in April, 2005.[76] Since the resumption of the peace process, Secretary level talks representing the Indian Ministry of Tourism and Culture and Pakistani Ministry of Culture were held on the "Promotion of Friendly Exchanges in Various Fields" in New Delhi, on 3-4 August 2004. Both sides discussed measures to liberalise visa regimes and expand the scope of the 1974 bilateral Protocol on Visits to religious shrines.[77] Humanitarian issues such as exchange of prisoners and disaster management figured in the discussions. In order to enhance cross-border movement of people to meet their long divided families and relatives India and Pakistan agreed to start a number of bus services including the one between Srinagar and

Muzaffarabad.[78] The opening of bus services and train routes has given more opportunities for people to meet their loved ones across the border. The visits of leaders and civil society members between both countries have contributed a great deal in relaxing the tensions. In particular, the emphasis of both governments to facilitate more exchanges in the fields of sports, arts and culture are expected to go a long way in furthering the peace process.

Notes

1. AshutoshMisra, "*An audit of the India-Pakistan peace process*", Australian Journal of International Affairs, Vol. 61, No. 4, Routledge, UK, 2007, p. 506.
2. *Ibid.*
3. Robert G. Wirsing, *Kashmir in the Shadow of War: Regional Rivalries in a Nuclear Age,* Spring Books Gurgaon, India, 2004, p. 17.
4. The two foreign secretaries agreed to discuss 'all outstanding issues of concern including, inter alia: (a) Peace and security, including CBMs, (b) Jammu and Kashmir, (c) Siachen, (d) Wullar Barrage Project/Tulbul Navigation Project, (e) Sir Creek, (f) Terrorism and drug-trafficking, (g) Economic and Commercial Cooperation (h) Promotion of friendly exchanges in various fields. It was decided that the first two issues would be dealt with at the level of Foreign Secretaries who will also coordinate and monitor the progress of work of all the working groups.
5. A.G. Noorani-I, "*India-Pakistan Peace Process*", Institute of Regional Studies, Seminar Papers, Islamabad, 20-21 Oct 2008, pp. 136-137.
5. Dr. Smruti S. Pattanaik, Dr Arpita Anan, "*Cross-LoC Confidence Building Measures between India and Pakistan: A Giant Leap or a Small Step towards Peace*?" Institute for Defence Studies and Analyses, Issue Brief, February 12, 2010.
6. Interview with Dr. Hameeda Nayeem, September 2009, Kashmir University, Srinagar. She believed that the BJP's decision to revise the Composite Dialogue was an attempt to find some place

in Indian history by resolving some contentious issues with Pakistan since the whole credit of Indian National Movement is taken by the Congress party.7. Joint Statement: President Musharraf and PM Vajpayee, *Islamabad, January 6, 2004.* **Retrieved from:** http://www.satp.org/satporgtp/countries/india/document/papers/indo_pak-6jan04.htm.

8. On the eve of Id-ul-Fitr, Pakistani Prime Minister Zafarullah Jamali announced a ceasefire offer to India along the International Border (IB) and the Line of Control (LoC) on 23 November, 2003. India proposes extension of the ceasefire along the Actual Ground Position Line (AGPL) in Siachen. Formal ceasefire between India and Pakistan along the International Border (IB), Line of Control (LoC) and the Actual Ground Position Line (AGPL) in Jammu and Kashmir began at the midnight of 25th November, 2003.
9. The Composite Dialogue process between India and Pakistan has been replacing enmity with amity. The peace process between India and Pakistan has been on a cordial path. Since the rapprochement began in April 2003, significant progress has been made in normalising relations between the belligerent neighbours. This began after then Indian Prime Minister A.B. Vajpayee's Srinagar statement in April, 2003. The goodwill gesture was well received by the then Prime Minister of Pakistan, Zafarullah Jamali. He responded positively not only rhetorically, but he also took practical initiatives to materialise the good will gesture. Consequently, diplomatic representation at the two capitals has been restored; a cease fire declared at the Siachen and LoC; road, rail and air links have been revived; delegations of businessmen, Members of Parliament, artists and poets have exchanged visits, and cricket ties resumed after a break of nearly a decade and a half. Above all, both sides' rulers and higher government officials met number of times to ameliorate India-Pakistan relations.
10. A.G. Noorani-I, *op. cit.,* p. 132.
11. Ashok K. Behuria, "India-Pakistan Relations: An Indian Narrative", *Pakistan Institute of Legislative Development and Transparency, (PILDAT)*, January 2011, Web: www.pildat.org.
12. Moonis Ahmar, *The Challenge of Confidence-Building in South Asia*, Har-Anand Publications, New Delhi, 2001, p. 416.

13. *Ibid.*
14. Pervaiz Iqbal Cheema-I, "*More Confidence Building Measures*", Pakistan Observer, Oct. 13, 2007.
15. Muhammad Irshad, "*Indo-Pak Confidence-Building Measures*", *Defence Journal,* Karachi, August, 2002. Retrieved from: http://www.defencejournal.com/2002/august/confidence.htm.
16. Pervaiz Iqbal Cheema-II, "The Contribution of Track-II towards India-Pakistan Relations", *South Asian Survey*, Vol. 13, New Delhi, September 2006, pp. 211-30.
17. *Ibid.*
18. *Ibid.*
19. Syed Hussain Shaheed Soherwordi, "CBMs and Peace in South Asia", *Defence Journal,* Karachi, August 2000. Retrieved from: http://www.defencejournal.com/2000/aug/cbms.htm
20. Pervaiz Iqbal Cheema-II, *op. cit.*, pp. 215-33.
21. *Ibid.*
22. *Ibid.*
23. Rizwan Zeb and Suba Chandran, *Indo-Pak Conflicts: Ripe to Resolve?* Regional Centre for Strategic Studies (RCSS) Colombo, Manohar Publishers and Distributors, New Delhi, 2005, p. 24.
24. Text of the joint statement made by Foreign Secretaries of India and Pakistan, *The Hindu*, 25 September, 1998.
25. Text of Lahore Declaration signed between the Prime Ministers of India and Pakistan on 21 February 1999. <http://www.nti.org/e_research/official_docs/inventory/pdfs/lahore.pdf>
26. Robert G. Wirsing, *op. cit.*, p. 58.
27. Rizwan Zeband Suba Chandran, *op. cit.*, p. 27.
28. C. Raja Mohan, "Fernandes Unveils 'Limited War' Doctrine," *The Hindu,* 25th January 2000.
29. Rizwan Zeband Suba Chandran, *op. cit.*, p. 30.
30. *Ibid.*
31. Ashok Sharma, "Indian PM offers friendship to Pakistan from behind bulletproof glass", *The Guardian,* 19th April 2003.

32. Amit Baruah, "India proposes a Dozen Steps to Break the Ice with Pak", *The Hindu*, 23rd October 2003.
33. Rizwan Zeb, "Recent Indo-Pak Offers: Old Wine in New Bottle?" *Institute of Regional Studies,* Islamabad, 27th November 2003. Retrieved from:http://www.ipcs.org/article/indo-pak/recent-indo-pak-offers-old-wine-in-new-bottle-1214.html
34. Kanti Bajpaiet al., *Kargil and After: Challenges for Indian Policy,* Har-Anand Publications, New Delhi, 2001, p. 198.
35. Samina Ahmad and Varun Sahni, "Freezing the Fighting: Military Disengagement on Siachen Glacier", Cooperative Monitoring Center Occasional Paper No. 1, Cooperative Monitoring Center, Sandia National Laboratories, Albuquerque, New Mexico, 1998, p. 10.
36. *Ibid.*
37. Kanti Bajpai, *op. cit.*, p. 200.
38. Samina Ahmad and Varun Sahni, *op. cit.*, p. 16.
39. *Ibid.*
40. Kanti Bajpai, op. cit., p. 201.
41. Samina Ahmad and Varun Sahni, *op. cit.*, p. 21.
42. *Ibid.*
43. Atul Aneja, "Siachen Accord Envisages a Thaw," *The Hindu,* March 28, 1997.
44. *Ibid.*
45. A.G. Noorani-II, "The Siachen impasse", *Frontline,* November 09, 2002.
46. Ashutosh Misra, *op. cit.*, p. 519.
47. Samarjit Ghosh, "Indo-Pak Composite Dialogue—2008: A Review", *Institute of Peace and Conflict Studies* (IPCS), Special Report 65, February, 2009.
48. Kanti Bajpai, *op. cit.*, p. 231.
49. Bharat Bhushan, "Tulbul, Sir Creek and Siachen: Competitive Methodologies", *South Asian Journal,* No.7 Jan-Mar 2005.
50. *Ibid.*

51. Kanti Bajpai, *op. cit.*, p. 235.
52. Ashutosh Misra, "The Sir Creek Boundary Dispute: A Victim of India-Pakistan Linkage Politics", *International Boundaries Research Unit (IBRU),* Boundary and Security Bulletin, UK, Winter 2000-2001, p. 91.
53. *Ibid.*
54. Bharat Bhushan, *op. cit.*, 2005.
55. *Ibid.*
56. *Ibid.*
57. Kanti Bajpai, *op. cit.*, p. 219.
58. Shaheen Akhtar, "War on Terrorism and Kashmir issue", *Institute of Regional Studies (IRS),* Islamabad, 2010. Retrieved from: http://pu.edu.pk/images/journal/pols/Currentissue-pdf/SHAHEEN %20AKHTAR.pdf
59. *Ibid.*
60. Pakistan-India Joint statement, *Dawn,* Karachi, January 7, 2004.
61. Rajen Harshe, "Cross-Border Terrorism: Road-Block to Peace Initiatives", *Economic and Political Weekly,* August 30, 2003, p. 3622.
62. *Ibid.*
63. *Ibid.*
64. Samarjit Ghosh, "Indo-Pak Composite Dialogue—2008: A Review", *Institute of Peace and Conflict Studies, (IPCS),* Special Report 65, February 2009.
65. Ranjit Singh Ghuman and Davinder Kumar Madaan, "Indo-Pakistan Trade Cooperation and SAARC", *Peace and Democracy in South Asia,* Vol. 2, No. 1, 2006, p. 72.
66. R.S. Ghuman, *Indo-Pakistan Trade Relations,* Deep and Deep Publications, New Delhi, 1986, p. 81.
67. Ranjit Singh Ghuman and Davinder Kumar Madaan., loc. cit.
68. *Ibid.*
69. Nabiha Gul, "Enhancing Indo-Pak Trade: Perspectives from Pakistan", *Institute of Peace and Conflict Studies,* Issue Brief 122, New Delhi, September, 2009, p. 2.
70. *Ibid.*

71. *Ibid.*
72. *Ibid.*
73. Pia Malhotra, "Enhancing Indo-Pak Trade: Perspectives from India", *Institute of Peace and Conflict Studies,* Issue Brief 119, New Delhi, September 2009, p. 2.
74. *Ibid.*
75. *Ibid.*
76. Ashutosh Misra, *op. cit.*, p. 521.
77. *Ibid.*
78. *Ibid.*

3

Mapping the Progress of the Composite Dialogue Process

The India-Pakistan Composite Dialogue, borne out of the 6th January 2004 joint statement given by Atal Behari Vajpayee and General Musharraf laid the ground for the formulation of the eight-point agenda that were detailed by the respective foreign secretaries in February 2004.[1] The following issues constitute the eight point Composite Dialogue: Peace and Security including CBMs, Jammu and Kashmir, Siachen, Wullar Barrage/Tulbul Navigation Project, Sir Creek, Terrorism and Drug Trafficking, Economic and Commercial Cooperation and Promotion of Friendly Exchanges in Various Fields. So far, four rounds of Composite Dialogue have been completed and the fifth one was inaugurated by the foreign secretaries in July 2008. Detailed exposition of the progress made in the aforementioned issues under the framework of Composite Dialogue is as follows:

1. Peace and Security including CBMs

Despite events precipitating increased tensions between the two countries, the effort on the part of both governments has been to ensure that the Confidence Building Measures (CBMs) continue to remain in place, to enable the people of both countries, in the border regions in general and in the state of Jammu and Kashmir in particular, to maintain a semblance of normalcy in their lives. However, the impressive range of

CBMs, both of a military and non-military nature, have been overtaken by events such as the Kargil conflict in 1999, the mobilisation of troops in 2002, and the repeated terrorist attacks in India.

The following may be considered as the major achievements of CBMs over the past two decades:

Military CBMs

1. Agreement on the Prohibition of Attack against Nuclear Installations and Facilities– Signed in 1988, and eventually ratified in 1992. This particular exchange has continued for 18 consecutive years. The agreement also included an informal accord of a moratorium on further testing.
2. Agreement on Advance Notification on Military Exercises, Manoeuvers and Troop Movements– Brought into effect in 1991 and has an important role to play in the reduction of tensions on both sides of the Line of Control.
3. Agreement on Prevention of Airspace Violations and for Permitting over flights and Landings by Military Aircrafts– Signed in 1991, has significantly reduced costs for both nations, and also brought into being a structure of redress in case of violations and mutual trust in matters of requirement.
4. Formal Ceasefire along the International Border as also the Actual Ground Position Line– Brought into effect at midnight of 25th November, 2003 and has remained in effect since.
5. Biannual Meetings between Indian Border Security Forces and Pakistani Rangers– Has been in effect since 2004, and there has been mutual agreement that local commanders should meet more frequently to resolve local problems.
6. Agreement on Advance Notification of Ballistic Missile Tests– Brought into effect in 2005 and required both parties to inform the other 72 hours in advance before testing any ballistic missiles within a 40 km radius of the International Border and the Line of Control.
7. Establishment of a Communication Link between Pakistan Maritime Security Agency and Indian Coast Guard– Brought into effect in

2005, primarily to facilitate early exchange of information regarding fishermen apprehended for straying into each other's waters. The agreement also brought into discussion the possibility of holding joint search and rescue operations and collaborating in marine pollution control.

8. A Hotline between Director Generals of Military Operations of both countries had been in effect since 1965, and was most recently used in an unscheduled exchange to discuss troop movements and allay tensions, in the aftermath of the 26/11 attacks in Mumbai.[2]

Non-Military CBMs

The predominant confidence building measures in the non-military domain have been travel measures to increase people-to-people interaction:

1. Delhi-Lahore bus service was started in 1999, but was stopped in light of the Kargil conflict. It was resumed in 2003;
2. Passenger and freight rail services between Attari and Lahore, and air linkages between the two countries were resumed in 2004;
3. The Samjhauta Express, which runs between Delhi and Lahore, resumed service in 2005, and despite the 2007 blasts, has continued to run since;
4. The first bus service between Srinagar and Muzaffarabad was started in 2005;
5. Bus services from Lahore to Amritsar, Amritsar to Nankana Sahib and train links between Munabao in Rajasthan and Khokhrapar in Sindh were started in 2006. Night bus service between Ferozepur and Fazikla to Ludhiana-Chandigarh was also resumed the same year;
6. The first overland truck route between the two countries was opened at the Wagah border crossing in 2007;
7. Air links were increased from 12 to 28 flights weekly, triple-entry permit for cross-LoC travel introduced and the frequency of the Srinagar-Muzaffarabad bus service increased from fortnightly to weekly, in 2008. Trade routes on the Wagah-A tari, Srinagar-Muzaffarabad and Poonch-Rawalakot road links, as also the

Munabao-Khokhrapar rail link were also opened up the same year;

8. Humanitarian aid in terms of food, medicine and the like was extended by India and accepted by Pakistan, in the aftermath of the earthquake in Pakistan in 2005;[3]
9. A Joint Anti-Terrorism Institutional Mechanism to identify and implement counter-terrorism initiatives and investigations in both countries was brought into effect in 2006;
10. An agreement facilitating regular contact between state-run think tanks, Institute of Defence Studies and Analyses (New Delhi), and Institute of Strategic Studies (Islamabad) was brought into being in 2008. This agreement is meant to contribute to building channels of communication at the level of scholars;
11. The first meeting of a Joint Judicial Committee of judges belonging to both countries was conducted in 2008. This committee is meant to look into the welfare and release of prisoners jailed in both countries. More than 500 prisoners have been released by both sides in repeated instances in 2003, 2004, 2005, 2007, 2008 and 2009;
12. Joint Economic Commissions and Joint Business Councils were reactivated in 2004;
13. Foreign Ministers of both countries agreed to a series of Kashmir-specific CBMs to facilitate crossing the LoC in 2008;
14. Both countries agreed to host festivals displaying each other's movies in 2006. The Pakistani Government allowed for the legal release of Indian films in Pakistan in 2008;
15. Government representatives of both countries have continued to meet over the years, despite troubling circumstances. Case in point is the meeting between Indian Prime Ministers Dr Manmohan Singh and his Pakistani counterpart Yousuf Raza Gilani in Egypt, and Foreign Ministers Krishna and Qureshi in New York in 2009.[4]

Goodwill gestures such as the decision to release all fishermen, as well as civilian prisoners whose national status was confirmed and who had completed their sentences, will help improve the bilateral environment. The decision to allow cross-border trade along the Srinagar-Muzaffarabad route should benefit Kashmiris on both sides of the LoC. Yet these and other CBMs will only be effective if implemented in earnest. For instance, export of fruit from the Kashmir valley to Muzaffarabad and Pakistan has been a longstanding Kashmiri demand. But if administrative constraints block the delivery of perishable goods, they would fuel resentment, just as constraints on cross-LoC travel, including clearances from Indian and Pakistani intelligence agencies, have undermined the effectiveness of that CBM.

2. Jammu and Kashmir

Stephen P. Cohen argues that 'Kashmir is the most important single conflict in the subcontinent, not just because its territory and its population are contested, but because larger issues of national identity and regional power balances are imbedded in it.[5] Solving the Kashmir dispute means addressing these larger concerns and they cannot be addressed without new thinking on Kashmir and Kashmiris. The Composite Dialogue promised to be different from previous negotiations by virtue of not making Jammu and Kashmir the only issue on the table, however, the centrality of Jammu and Kashmir and Siachen as an adjunct is undisputable. Hence parleys conducted over these issues have been forever guided by the history of the respective disputes, thus formulating value judgements of the respective interlocutors and the resultant viewpoints they hold over the issues. The complex history of the region, coupled with the current status of the region and the flexibility of options available as solutions to the sides is based on their respective national and local political mandates. Another unique aspect of these issues is that their resolution has been sought at different levels—official diplomatic parleys, "back channel" diplomacy conducted by specially appointed representatives or National Security Advisors and Track-II diplomacy.[6]

Joint Statement at Islamabad

General Musharraf's government made several efforts to convince India of his good intentions in early 2003. These efforts finally led to the then Indian Prime Minister Vajpayee extending his hand of friendship in April 2003. This was followed by a bilateral ceasefire on the LoC in November 2003. Musharraf tried his best to revive the peace process with

India by seeking to project a 'flexible' approach towards Kashmir. In a November 2003 interview with the BBC, Radio Urdu service (in its programme 'Talking Point') he called for 'patience, sincerity, and flexibility' and reintroduced his four-step approach to Kashmir, once he had tentatively put across during the Agra talks which offered to eliminate all options unacceptable to India, Pakistan, and the people of Kashmir, and then evolve a consensual solution. The four step proposal envisaged:[7]

1. Official talks commence;
2. Centrality of the Jammu and Kashmir dispute is acknowledged;
3. Any proposal unacceptable to any party or Kashmiris is taken off the table;
4. Best solution acceptable to the parties and the Kashmiris is taken.

In his interview with Reuters on December 18, 2003, General Musharraf went even further. He offered to set aside Pakistan's long-held position on Kashmir and go beyond the UN resolutions. This offer was hailed as a significant step by many observers.[8] Vajpayee and Musharraf signed a joint statement on the sidelines of the South Asian Association for Regional Cooperation (SAARC) Summit in Islamabad on January 6, 2004. The agreement was, in many ways, a restart of the Lahore process. Musharraf had come round to accept a process of composite dialogue, leaving aside his emphasis on the 'core issue' of Kashmir. The joint statement mentioned Indian concerns on terrorism very clearly. It said that "in order to take forward and sustain the dialogue process, violence, hostility and terrorism must be prevented", and went on to secure Musharraf's reassurance to Prime Minister Vajpayee "that he will not permit any territory under Pakistan's control to be used to support terrorism in any manner". It also said that the two leaders agreed to commence the process of the 'composite dialogue', and expressed their confidence that the resumption of the composite dialogue will lead to peaceful settlement of all bilateral issues, including Jammu and Kashmir, to the satisfaction of both sides.[9] Later that year, there was a change in the government in India and Musharraf met the new Prime Minister, Dr Manmohan Singh, in New York on September 24, 2004. The two leaders signed a joint statement and indicated that they would start looking into various options on Kashmir and take the peace process forward.

Thinking Kashmir: From Four-steps to Autonomy and Self-governance

Unlike Nawaz Sharif, Musharraf commanded enormous powers as both the president and army chief. He was now ready for his 'out-of-box' thinking and made some proposals, which were interpreted as 'flexible' by observers in Pakistan and outside. If one examines the course of India–Pakistan dialogue since the Islamabad Summit, during the time General Musharraf held absolute sway (until 2007), one observes at the outset that Musharraf tried desperately to put Kashmir on the fast track, by offering a slew of proposals both to start dialogue with India and to project himself as a flexible leader at the international level. It is believed that Musharraf's four-step proposal was discussed amongst the officials of both countries during the course of the composite dialogue. Musharraf took another step forward from his four-step approach on October 25, 2004, during the course of an *Iftar* party in Islamabad, when he talked about progressive demilitarisation of 'seven regions of Kashmir' to be developed as self-governing units under joint control or UN mandate.[10] Kashmir is divided into seven regions—five with India and two with Pakistan. The beauty of these regions is that they are still religion-based even if we consider them geographically. He said that the debate could be initiated in the context of a three-pronged discourse. First, identify the region at stake. Second, demilitarise it. Third, change its status. For changing the status, there were 'many options which could then be considered, and legal experts on both sides could then look at the pros and cons of ideas for joint control, UN mandates, condominiums, and so on'.[11] He also outlined that Pakistan was not ready to accept the LoC as a permanent border and India was also not ready to accept a religion-based solution.

In May 2005, Musharraf held that any final solution on Kashmir had to be acceptable to Pakistan, India, and the Kashmiris. There should be enough efforts to generate public debate and public support towards the final objective. Manmohan Singh responded on May 29, 2005, saying that the 'sky is the limit'–once the Indian position about what was not possible—had finally been understood by Pakistan.[12] In view of the suspicion in certain quarters in Pakistan that Musharraf's government might go for a secret understanding with India on Kashmir, a Pakistani

Foreign Office spokesperson reiterated Musharraf's position on November 28, 2005, and said, "Let me assure you that any proposal, any idea that emanates from the government of Pakistan, it is in consultation with and endorsement of the Kashmiri leadership on both sides of the Line of Control."[13] Answering another query about whether trade with India before the solution of the Kashmir issue did not involve a shift in Pakistan's Kashmir policy, the spokesperson, Ms Tasnim Aslam, stated: "that is not our policy. We have trade relations with India and we are also working within the framework of South Asia Free Trade Agreement (SAFTA)."[14]

On December 5, 2006, Musharraf further polished his proposal and reiterated that without changing boundaries, the borders and the LoC could be made irrelevant through staggered demilitarisation and autonomy or self-governance, with a joint supervision mechanism in Kashmir.[15] The last time one heard Musharraf raising the Kashmir issue was in February, 2007, a few days before he took what was a fatal decision, that of removing the Chief Justice of Pakistan. He was persuasive in his tone: 'Kashmir is ripe for resolution…Courage is needed to reconcile and shake hands and forget and forgive rather than go for confrontation. Both sides have to swallow their pride and step back.'[16]

While the official process of composite dialogue and Musharraf's 'thinking aloud' in the media continued between 2003 and 2007, an unofficial back channel was activated (very much like the Niaz Naik–R.K. Mishra talks during, 1997–1998) to discuss issues in an informal and more nuanced manner. The two principal envoys—for Pakistan, a college classmate of Musharraf named Tariq Aziz, and, for India, a Russia specialist named Satinder Lambah—were developing what diplomats refer to as a "non-paper" on Kashmir a text without names or signatures which can serve as a deniable but detailed basis for a deal.[17] To refine the non-paper, Musharraf relied intuitively on Tariq Aziz while his Indian counterparts include J.N. Dixit, Prime Minister's national-security adviser and Satinder Lambah. Altogether, there were about two dozen of hotel sessions between 2004 and early 2007. The non-paper drafted in early 2007, laid out several principles for a settlement. Kashmiris would be given special rights to move and trade freely on both sides of the Line of Control. Each of the former princely state's distinct regions would receive a measure of autonomy—details would be negotiated later. Providing that violence declined, each side would gradually withdraw its troops from the region. At some point, the Line of Control might be acknowledged by both governments as an international border. It is not clear how firm a commitment on a final border the negotiators were prepared to make, or how long it would all take; the people involved generally suggested a time line of about ten to fifteen years.[18] Indian Prime Minister Dr Manmohan Singh, in a significant revelation, for the first time, publicly acknowledged that secret envoys from the two countries had almost arrived at an agreed resolution to end the conflict in Kashmir. "At one time it appeared an important breakthrough was in sight. However, in Pakistan, General Pervez Musharraf had to make way for a different set of leaders. I think that led to the process not moving properly. However, I still believe that good relations between India and Pakistan are possible."[19] Thus the decline in Musharraf's popularity since March 2007, especially after his suspension of the chief justice of country's apex court, political situation in Pakistan worsened. As Musharraf battled for his survival, the back-channel talks lost their shine and were almost called off.

Internal Dialogue Process

The internal dialogue process between New Delhi and Srinagar is the other major step taken by India to seek political solution to the issue of Kashmir. On September 5, 2005, Hurriyat leaders met Indian Prime Minister, Dr Manmohan Singh. On February 17, 2006 the Prime Minister holds a meeting with Mohammed Yasin Malik, the Chairman of Jammu and Kashmir Liberation Front.[20] Similarly on May 3, 2006, Prime Minister had also held talks with separatist leaders of Hurriyat conference led by its chairman Mirwaiz Umar Farooq in New Delhi, the two sides seemed at comfortable positions after these discussions.[21] On January 2, 2006, a three member Hurriyat delegation also visited Pakistan. However, these meetings could not help Hurriyat to participate in the process of Round Table Conference's (RTC's) being held to resurrect internal mechanism for restoration of peace and normality in the state. Centre-Hurriyat talks were aimed at resurrecting an internal process of confidence building by the Indian state. This internal agenda is being worked out through the round table conferences organised since February, 2006. In May 2006, Indian

Prime Minister held the 2nd Round Table Conference in Srinagar at which five working groups were set up to produce ideas on how to move the Kashmir peace process forward.

These working groups were on:

1. Strengthening relations across the Line of Control (LoC);
2. Center-State Relations;
3. Good Governance;
4. Infrastructure and Economic Development; and
5. CBMs within Jammu and Kashmir, including for widows and orphans of violence, return of displaced persons, and return of people who crossed over during the insurgency.

Working Group on Confidence Building Measures in Jammu and Kashmir headed by Mohammad Hamid Ansari in its report called for the review and repeal of Armed *Forces Special Powers Act* (*AFSPA*) and *Disturbed Areas Act* (DAA), which curtail the extent of individual freedom and civil liberties and impinge upon the fundamental rights of the citizens of Jammu and Kashmir.[22] The working group on strengthening cross-LoC relationships, headed by M.K. Rasgotra, recommended for "a joint consultative group or committee of 10 members each of the legislatures of both sides may be constituted to exchange views periodically on social, economic, cultural and trade-related matters of mutual interests". N.C. Saxena's working group on good governance noted that the State Human Rights Commission requires strengthening, and also called for the creation of a high-powered committee, including political representatives and civil society members, for enforcing human rights. While C. Rangarajan's working group, on economic issues focused on the reconstruction of the existing infrastructure, and offered pragmatic suggestions for a bottom-up revival of the State's economy.[23]

At the end of the third round table conference in New Delhi held in April 2007, a consensus was made to set up a standing committee and a monitoring mechanism for ensuring implementation of the various suggestions made by the working groups on Jammu and Kashmir. Government has announced its willingness to implement the following major recommendations of these working groups.

- To increase cross-LoC movement of people and goods by easing the travel of people across LoC;
- Promotion of pilgrim tourism across Kashmir without travel permits for senior citizens and to increase exchange of goods and other local products through the LoC;
- To resolve the problems of refugees from West Pakistan, who migrated to Jammu and Kashmir in 1947 in a time bound manner;
- Financial assistance to the kith and kin of militants killed in police encounters and relief to widows and orphans and migrant Kashmiri Pandits.[24]

One of the major criticisms of the present process is that these efforts are more towards conflict management rather than conflict resolution, especially with regard to the resolution of Kashmir issue which in fact is central to India-Pakistan peace and stability. During this period, Pakistan's side also talked to Jammu and Kashmir-based Kashmiri parties, including the moderate faction of the APHC led by Mirwaiz Omar Farooq. This was seen in the Pugwash conference on Kashmir held from 28-29 April 2008 in Islamabad. Mehbooba Mufti, the leader of PDP also met with Pakistani leaders.

Ground Reality at Present

The change of government in Islamabad after the February, 2008 elections did not impair the pace of the talks. The two most prominent Pakistani leaders, Asif Ali Zardari and Nawaz Sharif, put their weight behind the peace process. Zardari went to the extent of saying that a solution to Kashmir could wait but there must be movement on other fronts like promoting trade, people to people contact, and a friendly relationship with India. In his interactions with the media, he said that he did not consider India an enemy and that there was a little Pakistani in every Indian and vice versa.[25] The fact that the Mumbai attacks of November 26–27, 2008 coincided with Pakistani Foreign Minister Shah Muhammad Quereshi's visit to India and took place just after he addressed the Indian media expressing his good intentions to pursue the ongoing peace process, confirms that such elements would continue to imperil the process of peace and understanding between India and Pakistan.

3. Siachen

Siachen Glacier, the highest battle field in the world, is one of the most inhospitable and glaciated regions of hostility. Originating in the Karakoram Ranges, the glacier is 76 kilometers long and varies in width between two to eight kilometers.[26] Hostile weather conditions bear fatal consequences for the troops in the area, as only three per cent of the Indian casualties have been caused by enemy firing. The rest 97 per cent succumb to altitude, weather, and terrain.[27] In the frozen wastes of Siachen, General Frost Bite kills hundreds of jawans in the never-ending battle which both armies wage against Nature. Siachen has almost been solved several times. It awaits no more than signatures on a piece of paper readied virtually 20 years ago between Prime Ministers Rajiv Gandhi and Benazir Bhutto.[28] Fortunately, guns have been silenced in the area since the ceasefire was effected in 2004.

Given the high human and financial tolls, and because the territory is of little strategic value, India and Pakistan have held a series of negotiations to resolve the dispute, but in the absence of political will these have achieved little, though they came close in 1989 and 1992. At the fifth round of defence secretary-level talks in June 1989, an understanding was reached "to work towards a comprehensive settlement, based on redeployment of forces to reduce the chances of conflict, avoidance of the use of force and the determination of future positions on the ground so as to conform with the Simla Agreement and to ensure durable peace in the Siachen area".[29] But India and Pakistan failed to sign it, largely due to India's domestic political compulsions. Elections were round the corner and Rajiv Gandhi's Congress regime was opposed to troop withdrawal in an election year.[30] Since then adverse slides in Indo-Pak relations, primarily due to militancy in Jammu and Kashmir, has lowered trust levels between the two parties negating any compromise solution in the dispute. Proposals on prospective solutions have ranged from demilitarisation, joint monitoring, to turning it into a peace park. The basic dispute at present hinges on India insisting on authentication of the current troops positions before any withdrawal is undertaken and Pakistan refusing the proposal fearing that it may amount to a formal acknowledgement of India's occupation of the current positions. In recent years, back channel diplomacy has rekindled hopes of a compromise. India of late has begun contemplating a withdrawal, unlike before, subject to assurances that vacated positions would not be re-occupied by Pakistan. Similarly, Pakistan has moved away from its insistence on an unconditional withdrawal and started to accommodate India's concern without undermining its own official stand on the dispute.[31] The talks on Siachen resumed at the Defence Secretary level in August 2004 which proved inclusive, apart from agreeing to hold further talks on the dispute. The Foreign Secretaries of India and Pakistan met on 4th September, 2004 in New Delhi again to discuss the eight baskets of issues including Siachen. These review talks were focused more on the progress made so far rather than discussing the technicalities involved in them. The Defence Secretaries level talks between India and Pakistan to discuss Siachen issue under the Composite Dialogue Framework were again held in Islamabad on 26-27 May 2005.[32] The Pakistan delegation was led by Defence Secretary Lt. Gen Tariq Waseem Ghazi (Retd.). The Indian delegation was headed by Defence Secretary Ajai Vikram Singh. The two sides held frank and constructive discussions with a view to taking the process forward. They expressed satisfaction at the ceasefire currently in place since November, 2003 and agreed to its continuation. In 2006, Defence Secretary level talks on Siachen were held on 22-23 May, in New Delhi again with no substantial progress made besides agreeing to continue with the ceasefire and holding further talks. The issue was again up for discussion during the Foreign Secretary level meetings on 14-15 November, 2006 in New Delhi. Again the basic contention over the authentication of troop positions on the glacier hampered any progress. In a recent significant development, Pakistan proposed a 'middle way'. It offered to 'acknowledge' the current position of the Indian troops rather than 'authenticate' it, which suggested a tacit acceptance of India's claim over Siachen.[33] The proposal is lying with the Indian government which is giving it serious consideration and discussing the technicalities involved in detail. As the two foreign secretaries met again at Islamabad in March, 2007, nothing substantive was achieved. The defence secretaries met at Islamabad on 6th and 7th April, to discuss Siachen and Sir Creek but failed to make any headway.

While offering a treaty of "peace, friendship and security" to Pakistan in March 2006, Prime Minister Manmohan Singh had hinted that issues like the dispute over the Siachen glacier region and the boundary dispute in Sir Creek could be resolved soon. Pakistan's Foreign Minister, Khurshid Ahmed Kasuri, has been claiming that discussions to demilitarise the Siachen conflict zone, as a prelude to a final agreement to extend the Line of Control (LoC) beyond map reference NJ 9842, have been proceeding slowly towards reaching an agreement. However, the Indian side has been reticent and Defence Minster A.K. Antony, who visited Siachen on 5th May, 2007, has gone so far as to say that there is no question of progress on demilitarisation unless Pakistan authenticates the forward positions of Indian troops.[34] Since September 2007, India has welcomed mountaineering and trekking expeditions to the forbidding glacial heights. The expeditions have been meant to show the international audience that Indian troops hold almost all dominating heights on the important Saltoro Ridge west of Siachen Glacier, and to show that Pakistani troops are not within 15 miles (24 km) of the 43.5-mile (76 km) Siachen Glacier. An October, 2008 trek was "being undertaken to send a message that every civilian with the help of military can visit this part of the country," a senior Indian army officer explained.

The civilian treks to Siachen started despite vehement protests from Pakistan which termed it India's tourism in 'disputed territory'. Pakistan conducts similar expeditions in nearby areas under its control with no requirement of a military liaison officer to accompany trekkers; their permit formalities are simpler, often taking just two weeks. Pakistan in 2008 did not lodge a formal protest against the treks and India too has also kept it a low key affair, with Indian Defence Minister A. K. Antony skipping the flagging off ceremony.[35]

Resolution of Siachen could be a big step towards building trust and confidence between India and Pakistan. The resolution of Siachen issue has also become a priority from ecological point of view. The army presence on Siachen is a major environmental issue in the world for two main reasons. First the anthropogenic factor in the recession and retreat of glaciers thus affecting the supply of water to the rivers originating from these glaciers and secondly due to the accumulation of huge debris. All this is destroying the pristine ecological balance of these landforms. The development of Siachen as a 'Peace Park' in fact, is very important CBM in removing the mistrust in India-Pakistan relations.[36]

4. Wullar Barrage/Tulbul Navigation Project

India and Pakistan disagree even on the name of this dispute. India refers to it as Tulbul Navigation Project whereas Pakistan calls it the Wullar Barrage. The Tulbul Navigation Project located on the Jhelum river in Jammu and Kashmir has been the bone of contention between both the countries since 1984 when India proposed to build a barrage at the mouth of Wullar lake, near Sopore town in the Kashmir Valley.[37] However, Pakistan alleged that the construction of a barrage would impede the flow of water to Pakistan. Moreover, in its opinion, it also constituted a violation of the Indus Water Treaty, 1960. India refuted these allegations and claimed that construction of the barrage would make the river navigable in lean months. Pakistan went to the Indus Water Commission in 1986, but failed to prove its case. India abandoned the construction work until an agreement was reached through direct talks and discussions. More than a dozen rounds of talks have already been held to resolve the issue but with a little progress.

The talks resumed at the secretary level between the India Ministry of Water and Power and the Pakistani Ministry of Water Resources on 29-30 July, 2004 in which the two sides looked at the issue in light of the provision of the Indus Water Treaty of 1960. The talks were cordial but failed to yield any breakthrough.[38] In 2005, the next round of talks between the two ministries looked into the dispute, laying down future courses of action but like the previous round no tangible solution emerged. It is important to highlight that the term 'Storage Project' has been added to the nomenclature at Pakistan insistence, making the technical name read as 'Wullar Barrage and Storage Project/Tulbul Navigation Project'.[39] Pointing to the storage utility of the barrage, Pakistan has argued that India had violated Article I (11) of the Treaty, which prohibits both parties from undertaking any 'man-made obstruction' that may cause change in the volume of the daily flow of waters unless it is of an insignificant amount. Further, Article III (4) specifically barred India from storing any water or to construct any storage works on the Western Rivers. Though the treaty permitted limited storage (not exceeding 10,000- acre ft.) for purposes of flood control, it prohibited storage of water for the purpose of impounding the waters of a stream.[40] On 22-23 June, 2006, secretary level delegations from both sides looked into the dispute using the Indus

Waters Treaty as the guiding principles for their exercise. There was no progress made and the dispute awaits further talks. Delegations of the two countries also met in New Delhi on 30-31 August, 2007 for discussions on the Wullar Barrage/Tulbul Navigation Project. The Indian delegation was led by Mrs Gauri Chatterji, Secretary, Ministry of Water Resources, Government of India and the Pakistan delegation was led by Mr Muhammad Ismail Qureshi, Secretary, Ministry of Water and Power, Government of Pakistan. The talks were held in a cordial and constructive atmosphere. The two sides further discussed their respective positions on the project and had a better appreciation of each other's views. The two sides emphasised the need for an early and amicable resolution of the issue in accordance with the provisions of the Indus Waters Treaty of 1960 for the socio-economic development of the peoples of the two countries. The Secretaries agreed to hold discussions including at technical-level on mutually acceptable dates. Both sides looked forward to the next round of talks under the Composite Dialogue with a view to resolving the issue at an early date. The Pakistan delegation also called on Prof Saifuddin Soz, Minister for Water Resources, Government of India.[41] The dispute is mainly a resource issue, but due to its location, i.e., in Jammu and Kashmir, it becomes a politically sensitive issue for both sides. Technically speaking the dispute is not intractable in nature and it is the linkage with the Kashmir issue which hinders any progress on the matter. This dispute can be resolved provided it can be de-linked from the larger issue of Kashmir and be treated as purely a resource dispute, as was done when the Indus Waters Treaty was signed in 1960.

5. Sir Creek

Sir Creek, a fluctuating tidal channel, is a sixty-mile-long estuary in the marshes of the Rann of Kutch between the Indian state of Gujarat and the Pakistani province of Sind. It forms part of the once disputed Rann of Kutch Area in the Western Sector of India, which was settled through the Indo-Pakistani Western Boundary Case Tribunal's Award on 19th February 1968.[42] The Tribunal excluded the Creek saying that it was out of its purview.

Pakistan claims that all the 17 creeks of Sind coast belong to it while India claims that at least half of the area of Sir Creek belongs to it. As per the 1925 demarcation, boundary was shown by a "green line" depicted on the eastern side of the creek. However, Indian contention is that the "green line" was simply an indicative line, and the boundary line should be defined by 'mid channel' of the creek. But Pakistan rejects Indian claim on the grounds that the notion of "mid-channel" is applicable only to navigable channels while this channel is not a navigable one.[43] So the present dispute hinges on the demarcation of the boundary from 'the mouth of Sir Creek to the top of Sir Creek' and from 'the top of the Sir Creek eastwards to a point (on land) designated as the Western Terminus.' The boundary thereafter has been fixed. The determination of the boundary in the Creek area remains under dispute due to differences over whether the creek falls under the '*Thalweg Principle*', which provides for making the mid-channel as the boundary. India argues that it is a navigable creek and hence '*Thalweg Principle*' is applicable, which is disputed by Pakistan. Pakistan says that the boundary lies on the eastern side and hence the creek is Pakistan's which in turn is disputed by India.[44] Determination of the boundary in the Creek area enlarges the Exclusive Economic Zone (EEZ) of either side by 250 sq. miles making it a territorial-cum-resource dispute, and hence the deadlock. Pakistan also insists that the boundary in the Creek first be delimited in order to establish the point on the land from which a sea boundary can be delimited.

India's concerns centre on the delimiting of the maritime boundary first and then moving towards the land. Both sides are keen to settle the dispute which would enable them to undertake oil and gas exploration.[45] Several rounds of talks have been held since 1989 to settle the matter but with a little success. In recent years, both sides have shown seriousness in settling the matter to escape the United Nations Convention on the Laws of the Sea (UNCLOS) which would declare the area as international waters should the two sides fail to determine their claims for respective maritime zones by 2009.[46] Realising this, both sides have undertaken concerted efforts to resolve the issue. In 2005, a joint survey was launched in the marshy strip by both the countries to ascertain their respective claims.[47] The survey covered the horizontal section of the creek. The second month-long survey took place in January 2007 in which hydrographers along with the ships of the two navies participated. The two surveys covered the land as well as the coast, to verify the outermost points of the coastlines in the disputed area, on the principle of equidistance.[48] Both the sides disagree on how to proceed forward in delineating the border. India's position on the issue is that the maritime boundary should be in the middle of the estuary, while Pakistan argues that the border should lie on the South-east bank. After the completion of the joint survey, officials on both sides had noted that there has been a convergence to a great degree among both the countries on the delineation of the boundary.

In May 2007, in the first formal meeting on this issue, under the fourth round of composite dialogue, both sides, led by the Surveyor General of India, Major General M. Gopal Rao and Additional Defence Secretary of Pakistan, Rear Admiral Tanveer Faiz, exchanged maps marked with their respective claims over the marshy area as well as the maritime boundary.[49] The two sides also explained the basis for their respective claims on the boundary. The officials on both sides have presented the outcome of their talks to their respective governments with their recommendations. On the other hand, the United Nations (UN) is keeping mum on the protracted dispute between India and Pakistan over the ownership of Sir Creek even after the expiry of the deadline on May, 2009 set by the world body to resolve this issue. The UN had set the deadline for both the archrival countries to resolve this dispute amicably with a warning that after the expiry of the deadline the disputed area of sea would convert into the international waters. The UN fixed this deadline in 1982, but after a lapse of 26 years, India and Pakistan have failed to settle this issue as a result of which the fishermen of both the countries are in serious trouble as they are being detained frequently and put into jails in violation of the UN laws while their boats are being impounded.[50]

6. Terrorism and Drug Trafficking

One of the driving factors for India to agree to a composite dialogue was to address the issue of terrorism. Under the rubric of Composite Dialogue process, the first round of secretary level talks representing the Indian Home Ministry and Pakistani Interior Ministry was held on 10-11 August, 2004. The talks showed the willingness of the two sides to jointly address terrorism and drug trafficking and called for the signing of a Memorandum of Understanding (MoU) to institutionalise their cooperation on these counts.[51] The two delegations also expressed their satisfaction over the growing cooperation between Narcotics Control Authorities of the two sides through information sharing. The second round of secretary level talks were held on 29-30 August, 2005 discussing the progress made since the first round and steps which could be taken to eliminate terrorism. In these talks the proposal for cooperation between the Indian Central Bureau of Investigation and Pakistani Federal Investigation Agency was considered as well.[52] The technical level talks were held between the Central Bureau of Investigation (Indian) and Pakistan's Federal Investigation Agency on 21-22 March, 2006 in New Delhi. These discussions were considered significant for being held after a span of 17 years and dealt with key security challenges such as human trafficking, counterfeit currency and illegal immigration. The third round of talks at the level of interior/home secretaries was held on 30-31 May, 2006 which praised the progress made in talks between the Indian Narcotics Control Bureau (NCB) and the Pakistani Anti Narcotic Force (ANF). The meeting between ANF and NCB to jointly address the threat of drug trafficking across the IB and LoC could be seen as significant and meaningful which shows that while the longstanding disputes still persist, the two sides can establish cooperation in addressing common challenges.[53]

Joint Anti-terrorism Mechanism (Havana Declaration)

Havana meeting of the Non Aligned Movement, in September, 2006 concluded on a positive note. Indian Prime Minister Manmohan Singh and Pakistan President General Pervez Musharraf emphasised that the peace process must be maintained and its success was important for both the countries. This marked a resumption of the derailed Indo-Pak composite dialogue process following the 11th July, 2006 Mumbai multiple train blasts.[54] Both sides resolved to create a joint institutional mechanism to identify and implement counter-terrorism initiatives and investigations. This marked a new beginning to tackle terrorism as a "collective threat" in the Indo-Pak equation. It was a bold step to move beyond finger pointing through media and engage directly through an institutional framework. The first meeting of JATM (March, 2007) was held in the backdrop of tragic Samjhauta Express incident and defined the parameters of bilateral anti-terror co-operation. This meeting defined the framework of the mechanism and agreed that specific information to be exchanged for helping investigations on either side related to terrorist acts and prevention of violence and terror acts in the two countries.[55] It was also agreed that while the anti-terrorism mechanism would meet on quarterly basis, any information which is required to be provided on priority basis would be immediately conveyed to the respective heads of the mechanism. Second meeting of the JATM (October 22, 2007) led to the update on the information shared in the earlier meeting and resolved to cooperate with one another to identify measures, exchange specific information and assist in investigations. However, prior to the meeting, both sides traded accusatory remarks about subversive activities within their respective borders. Pakistan's foreign spokesperson said: "We had indications of Indian involvement with anti-state elements in Pakistan". On the Indian side, National Security Adviser M.K. Naraynan charged Pakistan, "for building up and stirring Sikh militancy in northern Punjab State".[56] India also blamed the ISI for bomb blasts in Hyderabad, Ajmer, and Ludhiana. This love and hate relationship continued and till the third and last meeting of joint anti-terror mechanism was held in Islamabad on June 28, 2008 in the backdrop of the Kabul blast of Indian Embassy. Both sides exchanged fresh information about terrorist incidents including, Samjhauta Express.

On the other hand, the fourth round of Home/Interior Secretary Level Talks between India and Pakistan on Terrorism and Drugs Trafficking, as a part of the continuing Composite Dialogue process between the two countries, was held in New Delhi on July 3, 2007. The Indian delegation was led by Shri Madhukar Gupta, Union Home Secretary while the Pakistan delegation was headed by Syed Kamal Shah, Secretary, Ministry of Interior.[57] Both sides strongly condemned all acts of terrorism and underlined the imperative need for effective and sustained measures against terrorist activities. Both sides welcomed the release of prisoners and fishermen by each other on the eve of these Talks as a gesture of goodwill and on humane considerations. They also agreed to release by August 14-15, 2007, those prisoners who have been granted consular access, whose national status has been verified and who have completed their prison sentences. The two sides also agreed to release by August 14-15, 2007 the remaining fishermen in each other's custody on completion of due process. Both sides noted with satisfaction that the recently formed Committee on Prisoners, comprising eminent retired judges from the two countries, is a useful instrument to facilitate release and repatriation of prisoners who have served their prison sentences. Separate working groups discussed in detail the drafts of the revised Visa and Consular Access Agreements aimed at liberalising and making existing provisions more effective. The text of the Agreement on Consular Access has been finalised. Also, they made considerable progress towards early finalisation and signing of the Visa Agreement. Both sides assessed as positive the existing cooperation and information sharing between the Narcotics Control Bureau of India and the Anti-Narcotics Force of Pakistan and agreed that both Agencies would enhance mutual cooperation in terms of effective and sustained steps to control drugs trafficking. The nodal points in both Agencies will meet periodically to facilitate early disposal of Interpol related cases. It was agreed to continue the discussions within the framework of the Composite Dialogue.[58]

The fifth round of Interior/Home Secretary Level Talks between India and Pakistan on Terrorism and Drugs Trafficking was held in Islamabad on 25th and 26th, November 2008 as a part of the Composite Dialogue. The Pakistan delegation was led by Syed Kamal Shah, Secretary, Ministry of Interior, while the Indian delegation was headed by Mr Madhukar Gupta, Home Secretary of India.[59] Both sides discussed the issues related to terrorism and drug trafficking and reviewed the implementation of decisions taken during the last round. They condemned terrorism in all its forms and manifestations and affirmed their resolve to co-operate with each other to combat the menace of terrorism. The MoU on Drug Demand Reduction and Prevention of Illicit Trafficking in Narcotics Drugs/Psychotropic Substances and Precursor Chemicals and Related Matters, was initialed. Both sides welcomed this development and agreed that the MoU will further promote bilateral co-operation in this field. It was agreed that Director General ANF of Pakistan and Director General of NCB of India will meet as early as possible to discuss ways of furthering cooperation. It was decided that the Federal Investigation Agency of Pakistan and the Central Bureau of Investigation of India will schedule a meeting at an early date to discuss ways of cooperation in addressing the issues of human trafficking, illegal immigration, and counterfeit currency, along with Red Corner Notices (RCN) subjects. It was agreed to continue the discussions within the framework of the Composite Dialogue. However, on 26th November, 2008, a group of terrorists, traced to Pakistan, attacked several key places in Mumbai – the Taj and the Oberoi hotels, among other places. It seemed that a war could break out between these two nuclear weapons upstarts. Thanks to the restraint exercised by their governments as well as hectic diplomacy by the United States (US), the United Kingdom and other major players, a major disaster was averted.[60] But India suspended the composite dialogue process since then and refused to revive it till such time that the perpetrators of the Mumbai attacks were arrested and put on trial.

6. Economic and Commercial Cooperation

The healthy trade relations between India and Pakistan got severe setbacks in the aftermath of wars of 1947-48, 1965 and 1971. The signing of bilateral trade agreement in January 1975 somehow restored trade engagements at government to government level. However, this agreement lasted for three years and could not be revived thereafter.[61] In March, 1983, India-Pakistan Joint Commission (IPJC) was established to build co-operation in different areas of inter-state relations.[62] The commission held its first meeting in June 1983. Under IPJC four sub-commissions were established in order to promote mutual co-operation in the areas of economics, health, science and technology, sports, travel, tourism and consular matters. In July 1989, India-Pakistan Joint Business Council was set up in the aftermath of third meeting of India-Pakistan Joint commission. After the Lahore Declaration, India-Pakistan Chamber of Commerce and Industry was established on April 10, 1999 to identify the major roadblocks to economic co-operation and to broaden their economic engagements to include collaboration in the areas of banking, insurance, medical, travel and human resource development.[63] However, despite all these efforts, the overall extent of bilateral trade between India and Pakistan remained abysmally low.

The Composite Dialogue Process (CDP) has led to substantial improvements in political relations over the last five years and trade relations have shown positive outcomes as well. In this regard, the Commerce Secretaries of the two sides met on 11-12 August 2004 in Islamabad to discuss various proposals to expand their economic and commercial relationship. The India-Pakistan Joint Study Group (JSG) which has been constituted to discuss trade and economic issues in a detailed manner met on 22-23 February, 2005. The delegation was led by the commerce secretaries of both sides.[64] The JSG constituted two Working/Sub Groups on Customs Cooperation and Trade facilitation and Non-Tariff Barriers (NTBs) and mutually agreed upon the Terms of Reference (TOR) for the Sub Groups. The first round of talks *per se* was held on 8-10 August, 2005 covering issues such as air services and air trade, shipping protocol and sea trade, a fibre optic link between Amritsar and Lahore and existing Non-Tariff Barriers among others. The second round of talks on Economic and Commercial Cooperation was held on 9-10 August, 2005. The two sides agreed that the aeronautical talks would be held in Pakistan in September, 2005 to review the existing Air Services Agreement, bilateral meeting to review the Shipping Protocol of 1975 would also be held in Pakistan in September, 2005 and the second meeting of the Joint Study Group (JSG) would be convened at an early date in Islamabad. The JSG meeting would be preceded by the meeting of the Sub- Groups on Non-Tariff Barriers (NTBs) and Customs Cooperation and Trade Facilitation to formulate recommendations for consideration by the JSG.[65] The third round of Economic and Commercial co-operation was held on 28-29 March, 2006 at Islamabad. A broad range of issues were discussed from opening of scheduled branches of banks in each country, tea trade, shipping procedures, problems of transportation of goods to enlargement of export items from India to Pakistan and the feasibility of trade in IT-enabled medical services. Both sides expressed satisfaction over the ratification of the South Asian Free Trade Agreement (SAFTA) by all SAARC member states which can potentially boost intraregional trade to a great extent.[66]

The Fourth Round of India-Pakistan talks on Economic and Commercial Cooperation within the framework of the Composite Dialogue was held on 31st July–1 August, 2007 in New Delhi. The Indian delegation was led by Commerce Secretary, Shri G.K. Pillai and the Pakistani delegation was led by Syed Asif Shah, Secretary of Ministry of Commerce.[67] The talks were held in a cordial and constructive atmosphere.

The two sides agreed on the following :

1. Both sides emphasised the importance of having bank branches in either country to facilitate trade. Both sides agreed to finalise

the processing of the applications for the two bank branches in either country within six months of the receipt of applications or by 31st December, 2007 whichever is later;

2. To facilitate import of cement from Pakistan, the Indian side informed that India will complete all statutory certification related formalities on a fast track. The Indian side informed that it is also in the process of making appropriate policy changes to accept third party certification;
3. To facilitate import of tea from India it was agreed to facilitate and encourage the trading of tea through rail. Pakistan side noted the request for providing duty concessions on import of Indian tea;
4. Pakistan will nominate representatives to the Joint Working Group to discuss the issues relating to joint registration of Basmati rice as Geographical Indication (GI) and the first meeting of the Group will be held at an early date. The Pakistan side raised the issue of Notification issued by India declaring 'Super Basmati Rice' as an approved variety for export. India agreed to look into this issue;
5. The Indian delegation handed over a list of 484 tariff lines for inclusion in the Positive List of items importable from India. The Pakistan side agreed to examine the request in consultation with stakeholders;
6. The Indian side informed that a Task Force comprising of representatives from various ministries and departments of Government of India has been constituted to address the issues of Non-Tariff Barriers (NTBs) and para-tariffs. The Task Force will make recommendations in a time bound manner for removing these barriers to provide greater market access to all members of SAARC;
7. In order to address the issue of imbalance in bilateral trade, the Indian side invited the Pakistan side to identify twenty products of its export interest so that India could inform Pakistan about the detailed import regime on these products with a view to facilitating their import into India;
8. Both sides will facilitate holding of trade exhibitions in each other's country. The Indian side invited Pakistan to organise a "Made in Pakistan" Trade Fair in India;

9. A delegation from Pakistan was invited to visit India to see some of the IT-enabled tele-medicine facilities, with the objective of exploring avenues of cooperation in this field;
10. The Indian side made a presentation on the state of development of Integrated Check-post (ICP) planned to be developed at Wagah/Attari Border at the Indian side. The Pakistan side also briefed on the state of infrastructure and proposed plan for development on its side. Both sides agreed to continue the exchange of information on the development of ICPs on either side;
11. Both sides noted with satisfaction the initiative to allow cross border movement of trucks, up to designated points at Wagah/Attari, for unloading/reloading of cargo. It was decided that the first technical level meeting to work out modalities would be held on 20th August, 2007 at the Wagah border on the Pakistan side;
12. Indian side also proposed that in order to reduce pressure on Attari-Lahore Rail route and to improve trade, the Munabao-Khokrapar route should be opened for freight movement. Pakistan side noted the proposal;
13. Both sides agreed to constitute a Joint Group headed by Joint Secretaries of Commerce of both countries to monitor and coordinate the decisions taken during the Fourth Round of talks on economic and commercial cooperation within the framework of Composite Dialogue.[68]

The fifth phase of the composite dialogue took place in July 2008, under the shadow of the suicide attack on the Indian embassy in Kabul, which left a number of Afghans and Indians, including a civil servant and a military dead and several others injured. This was unarguably the lowest point in Indo-Pak relations in the past four years. The American intelligence agencies had claimed that the Inter-Services Intelligence (ISI) agency of Pakistan had a hand in the attack.[69] It was difficult then for India to resume the composite dialogue, as the Kabul suicide attack was followed by terrorist attacks in Ahmadabad and New Delhi. On the fateful night of 26th November, 2008, Pranab Mukherjee and Shah Mehmood Qureshi had spoken about boosting trade relations, people-to-people contacts and combating terrorists together. The Indian government was also considering sending the Indian cricket team to tour Pakistan, a move which has always served as a popular track-two measure. However, the Mumbai terror attacks on 26-29 November, the financial capital of India, have seriously affected all dimensions of relations between the two countries for the foreseeable future. The composite dialogue process has therefore frozen, the first casualty being the trade talks, an area where the civilian government in Islamabad had shown great enthusiasm. India called off a prospective visit by a team from the Planning Commission, which was intended to facilitate an eventual visit by Deputy Chairman, Montek Singh Ahluwalia, who would have been returning an earlier visit by his Pakistani counterpart, Salman Faruqui.[70]

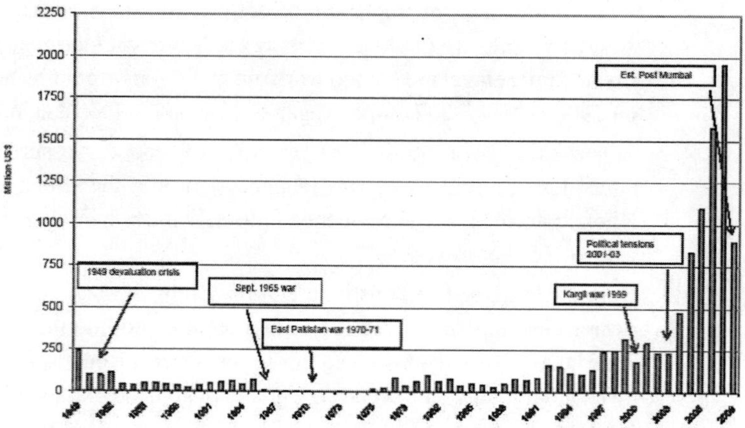

Fig. 1. Impact of Political Tensions on India-Political Trade.[71]
Note: *Trade is measured as a sum of exports and imports in nominal U.S. dollar values.*

One positive development in recent months has been the Indo-Pak rapprochement on the trade front. Given the history of mutual suspicion, the February 13, 2012 visit of Indian Commerce Minister Anand Sharma to Pakistan, the first in 30 years and at the head of an 80-strong business delegation, can arguably be termed as a success. In a potential paradigm shift in bilateral ties, Pakistan has agreed with India to adopt the "India-China model" in negotiating their sensitive relationship, which entails focusing on scaling up trade while resolving outstanding issues in a "step-by-step" incremental manner.[72] Trade fairs were held in Lahore and New Delhi with great fanfare. The inauguration of the Integrated Check

Post (ICP) at Attari in India on April 13, 2012 is important for a number of reasons. Built at a cost of nearly Rs. 150 crore and spread over about 130 acres, the ICP will have passenger and cargo terminals, security and scanning equipment, and passenger amenities, besides waiting areas, restaurants, duty-free shops, banks and other financial services. The ICP can handle about 600 trucks at a time. As a consequence of this enhanced infrastructural capability, trade, earlier conducted only between 8 a.m. and 4 p.m. can now stretch to 12 hours — between 7 am and 7 pm. Thus, more trucks can drive to India and cross over to Pakistan every day.

From the border at Attari Chief Minister of Indian Punjab Mr Prakash Singh Badal underlined Punjab's expansive interests in reconciliation with Pakistan. He said, "I am desperately waiting for the day when people of both the Punjabs would freely move across the borders without visa restrictions. All of us ardently wish that these physical barriers in the form of borders must be abolished forthwith to further cement the age-old socio-cultural and emotional ties between both the countries."[73] Mr Badal's call for a paradigm shift in relations with Pakistan highlights the huge disconnect between New Delhi's national security elite which talks to itself and the imperatives for regional cooperation in India's western provinces. Mr Badal's Baisakhi speech on the benefits of engaging Pakistan is not the only local narrative that questions the presumptions of the national security elite. Regional interests in trans-border cooperation with Pakistan from Kashmir to Kutch are demanding New Delhi to reframe its frontier policies.

Cross-LoC Trade

In 2006, an understanding was reached between India and Pakistan to start cross-LoC trade in Jammu and Kashmir. The Foreign Ministers of both countries met on May 21, 2008 to discuss new and existing Kashmir-specific Confidence Building Measures (CBMs), and agreed to increase the frequency of Srinagar-Muzaffarabad and Poonch-Rawalakote Bus services and allow intra-Kashmir trade and truck services. On July 18, 2008, the India-Pakistan Joint Working Group on cross-LoC CBMs met in Islamabad to simplify the procedure for issuing cross-LoC travel permits; to increase the frequency of the Srinagar-Muzaffarabad bus service; to launch a postal service between the two cities; and discussed the list of items to be allowed for trade through the truck service. On September 22, 2008, the modalities regarding the movement of trucks, code of conduct for the drivers, permits, security, timings and list of items to be traded were agreed upon between India and Pakistan to conduct cross-LoC trade. Following this, cross-LoC trade on the Srinagar-Muzaffarabad and Poonch–Rawalakote routes commenced from October 21, 2008. Twenty-one items were identified for duty free passage from each side. The 21 items approved for import and export include carpets, shawls, namdas, gabbas, embroidery items, fruits, vegetables, dry fruits, saffron, imli, rajmash, kashmiri spices, foam mattresses, medicinal herbs, janamaz, tasbihs, precious stones, peshawarichappal, maize, maize products, honey and rice.[74]

The mainstream Kashmiri political parties on both sides of the LoC and majority of the APHC leaders supported the reopening of the Srinagar-Muzaffarabad road for trade as it would provide an alternative trade route to ensure uninterrupted flow of consumer items into the valley and for exporting fruit and other items from there. The business and trade community across the LoC welcomed the beginning of trans-LoC trade. They felt that trade would bring the people closer across the LoC and reduce tension between the two countries while strengthening the peace process. However, traders face considerable obstacles, primarily from the heavy constraints that govern their activities. Whilst restrictions remain in force, traders across the LoC are limited to barter and therefore will be unable to fulfill the economic and peace building potential of the trade.

During the meeting of foreign Ministers of India and Pakistan on 27th July, 2011, the issue of cross-LoC trade and trade facilitation for Jammu and Kashmir was discussed. A few CBMs on Kashmir were expectedly announced after this meeting. The outcome was underwhelming and far lesser than the expectations. It has been making a news for long that some CBMs could include starting a Kargil-Skardu bus, increasing the frequency of the Srinagar-Muzaffarabad bus, a banking mechanism to replace the existing barter system, enhancing the list of items allowed to be traded, and increasing the number of trading days from two to four every week. While the list of CBMs, as laid out in the Joint Statement, does sound rather long, most of it is full of promises. There are, in fact, only two concrete measures among the list:

(i) The number of trading days stands enhanced from two to four days per week. Truck movements shall take place on Tuesdays, Wednesdays, Thursdays and Fridays, both on Srinagar-Muzaffarabad and Poonch-Rawalakot routes;.

(ii) Both sides will expedite the processing time for applications, which shall not be more than 45 days.[75]

Through a fully active cross-LoC trade, it is possible to develop the stagnated and backward economy of the state and free it from its dependency. The borders, which have so far played an obstructionist role, making it landlocked, will on the contrary help boost economic growth and make it dynamic. In three different but related ways, cross-LoC trade will contribute to the economy in Jammu and Kashmir. First, the economic activities of the local traders will be augmented and they could also explore alternative markets across the LoC. Second, trade activities in the long run would not be limited to traders within J&K but would involve those from other areas in India and Pakistan. Once trade interests are entrenched across the borders, the political hostilities would become gradually irrelevant. The state which is known as the 'nuclear flashpoint', could become the 'economic and trade flashpoint' between India and Pakistan. Rather than remaining a source of conflict between the two countries, it will become a bridge between the two. This in itself will change the character of the economy of the state. Many problems of the state's economy arise from its conflict-ridden status. Once the role of the state reverses from being a 'problematic' to an economically active zone between India and Pakistan, it will be able to receive all the benefits of liberalisation and globalisation. Private investment will be forthcoming and financial institutions will not be shy of investing. Finally, generating this kind of economic activity will help the state fully explore its trade and industrial potential. Industries with potential for immediate growth in Kashmir include the furniture industry–especially walnut wood furniture; horticulture–especially fruit processing; and floriculture. There is also a huge manufacturing sector located in Jammu, which will be boosted. Once trade relations are properly established, it would make way for further cooperative measures between the two sides of Jammu and Kashmir across the LoC. The Working Group on Strengthening the Cross-LoC Relations has recommended a number of joint activities that can be undertaken by both sides. It also talks about exploring 'scope for co-operation on subjects of common interest like environment protection, water management, natural disaster management and forestry'. Suggestions have also been made about joint tourism and power projects. Since the Hydel power projects in the J&K often become controversial issues between India and Pakistan, the option of joint venture projects among the stake holders from both sides of J&K can be explored to benefit population on both sides. Similarly, joint venture projects can be established in mining sector as there are huge mining reserves in the area of LoC spread across both sides of J&K.

Iran–Pakistan–India Gas Pipeline

The energy demands in both India and Pakistan are rising at a rapid pace with the increase in their populations and economic growth rates. Recently, the two countries agreed upon, Iran-Pakistan-India gas pipeline. In fact, Pakistan's decision to go ahead with this project, leaving aside the traditional reservations, points towards an element of rationality with regard to the issue of trade and economic re-engagements in South Asia.[76] In a public announcement, the former prime minister of Pakistan, Shaukat Aziz, declared the agreement on Iran-Pakistan-India gas pipeline as the reflection of "Pakistan's new approach towards its relations with India" and a step towards creating interdependency between the two economies.[77] The co-operation on this project is characterised as the most significant confidence building measure between the two sides in context of the ongoing process of normalisation of Indo-Pak ties.

8. Promotion of Friendly Exchanges in Various Fields

Since the resumption of the Composite Dialogue process, Secretary level talks representing the Indian Ministry of Tourism and Culture and Pakistani Ministry of Culture were held on the "Promotion of Friendly Exchanges in Various Fields" in New Delhi, on 3-4 August 2004.[78] Both sides discussed measures to liberalise visa regimes and expand the scope of the 1974 bilateral Protocol on visits to religious shrines. Humanitarian issues such as exchange of prisoners and disaster management figured in the discussions. The next round of meetings was held on 26-27 July, 2005 in Islamabad. On 1-2 June 2006, the third round of Secretary-level talks between India and Pakistan were held in New Delhi. Badal K. Das, Secretary, Department of Culture, Ministry of Tourism and Culture represented the Indian side and Jalil Abbas, Secretary; Ministry of Culture represented the Pakistani side.[79] They reviewed the progress in the field of Friendly Exchanges and looked at issues such as raising the number of pilgrims who seek to visit religious shrines on both sides and easing visa regulations for delegations and individuals who want to visit their relatives on both sides.

Meeting Points along the LoC

In 2005, India and Pakistan agreed to open five meeting points across the LoC for divided families, trade, pilgrimages and cultural interaction. These points are Rawalakot-Poonch (7, November), Chakothi-Uri (9 November), Nauseri-Tithwal (10 November), Tattapani-Mendhar (15 November) and Hajipur-Uri (16 November).[80] The technical level talks to enhance interaction and cooperation across the LoC were held in New Delhi on 2-3 May, 2006 which reviewed the operationalisation of the Srinagar-Muzaffarabad bus service (bus for peace) since it began in April, 2005. The meeting also discussed problems with the terribly slow application process for travel on the bus. This has been a major concern of travellers who confront long delays in clearance of their applications.

Transport Links

In order to enhance cross-border movement of people to meet their long divided families and relatives, India and Pakistan agreed to start a number of bus services. These included Srinagar-Muzaffarabad which started on 7th April, 2005, Poonch-Rawalakot on June 19, 2005 and Amritsar-Nankana Sahib on January 20, 2006. It has also been agreed to start truck trade on the Srinagar-Muzaffarabad and Suchetgarh-Sialkot. In addition, the Delhi-Lahore train service resumed on 11th July, 2003 (suspended in December 2001 following the terrorist attack on the Indian Parliament) and Kokhrapar-Munabao service on 18th February, 2006 (defunct since the 1965 war).[81] The Srinagar-Muzaffarabad bus service was a watershed in Indo-Pak relations. Initially, the talks were stalled over the modalities pertaining to travel documents with Pakistan insisting on United Nations documents and India on passports as travel documents.

Pakistan also demanded the bus service be limited to Kashmiris, as opposed to India's proposal to open it for all Indians. Eventually in February, 2005 in Islamabad, the two Foreign Ministers Nawtar Singh and Khursheed Mahmud Kasuri signed the agreement overcoming the differences on travel documents and domicile of the passengers. The bus service was inaugurated on 7th April 2005 but was opposed by political parties in Pakistan such the Pakistan Muslim League-Nawaz (PML-N) and Jamaat-e-Islami (JI) who argued it would dilute the 'core' issue of Kashmir.[83]

Fig. Inauguration of Srinagar-Muzaffarabad Bus Service by the Indian Prime Minister, Dr. Manmohan Singh in 2005.

On 2nd June, 2005 moderates belonging to the All Party Hurriyat Conference (APHC) in Jammu and Kashmir led by its Chairman Mirwaiz Umar Farooq boarded the bus to visit leaders in POK and Islamabad. The visit drew flak from the United Jihad Council (UJC) leader Syed Salahuddin and hardliners in Srinagar, with an unfazed Mirwaiz criticising the hardliners on both sides saying:[83]

> "For fear of being labelled as treacherous should we sit at home and repeat the song of UN resolutions. One lakh people have already lost their lives. Should we wait for the sacrifices of another lakh people before we begin to look at the other possible ways to resolve the issue? There are people in Kashmir who considered talking to

> New Delhi as treachery. Now, we are being told that even visiting Pakistan amounted to treachery. It is high-time the word treachery is re-defined...when we return to Kashmir, we need to redefine certain things...certain words and phrases."

The composite dialogue process has not been a total failure and has provided dividends to both sides which could not have accrued otherwise. For instance, conventional and nuclear CBMs have helped India and Pakistan keep mutual mistrust at bay through periodic contacts and information exchange. Similarly, transport links, meeting points along the LoC, cease-fire declarations along the LoC, IB, and AGPL, increased trade flows, movement of people across the border, friendly exchanges between professionals, academicians, journalists, NGOs, educational institutions and parliamentary delegations have helped to improve the atmosphere drastically. With regard to Jammu and Kashmir, both sides have shown an accommodative approach in terms of effecting people-oriented measures. The bus services and LoC meeting points to bring divided families together after 30-40 years has done a world of good to the local people and Indo-Pak ties. The APHC representatives from Jammu and Kashmir have supported the Indo-Pak talks and have played a key role as well, by travelling to Pakistan and discussing ideas and issues with the leaders in POK and Islamabad. The evolution of a spirit of compromise on all sides about making borders irrelevant rather than meaningful resulted from numerous rounds of discussion under the rubric of composite dialogue. The agreement over the Srinagar-Muzaffarabad bus service symbolised a growing convergence in the stance of India and Pakistan on Jammu and Kashmir. It showed that their proclamations on Jammu and Kashmir were not mere rhetoric and they did possess the capacities to make compromises in the larger interests of the people. This can be regarded as the most striking and significant change to have come about in their mindsets after decades of bitter animosity.

The issues of Siachen, Sir Creek and Tulbul/Wullar projects after numerous rounds of talks appear less intractable now than they were five years ago. In Sir Creek, Indo-Pak joint survey of the boundary pillars is complete and there remain no serious hindrances in its resolution which would benefit both countries. Similarly, the Siachen glacier dispute too, has drifted closer to a mutually agreed solution. The willingness on both sides to accommodate mutual concerns to effect troop withdrawal and possibly of making Siachen a no-man's land, or a prospective peace park or a zone for joint research and activities are fairly strong. The Tulbul/ Wullar project though has failed to make any headway in real terms, the discussion on various aspects suggest that it is all but a zero-sum game and therefore likely to be resolved amicably as progress in other disputes is made. In sum, the change in mindset on Jammu and Kashmir has been percolating down into Siachen, Sir Creek and Tulbul/Wullar disputes making them ripe for resolution much earlier than expected.

As economics gained eminence in defining and shaping bilateral relationships in the globalised world, India's huge market offers vast opportunities to the smaller economies of South Asian neighbours. The increase in trade volume between India and Pakistan shows the influence of commerce and trade in bolstering bilateral relations. It also denotes a transformation in Pakistan's perceptions of India's rise. As India's ties with the US, China and other major countries continues to grow impressively, its rise as an Asian power drives Pakistan to settle its disputes before the power asymmetry grows any further. A much stronger India in the next eight to ten years would be less vulnerable to bullying and pressures. This explains why old ideas, thinking and mindsets are being replaced by new ones to provide sustenance to the peace process and exploit the window of opportunity.

Notes

1. K.S. Manjunath et al., "Indo-Pak Composite Dialogue 2004-05: A Profile", *Institute of Peace and Conflict Studies,* New Delhi, Special Report 12, February, 2006. Retrieved from: http://www.ipcs.org/pdf_file/issue/1372586579IPCS-Special-Report-12.pdf.
2. Samarjit Ghosh, "Two Decades of Indo-Pak CBMs: A Critique from India", *Institute of Peace and Conflict Studies,* New Delhi, Issue Brief 132, September 2009, p. 2.
3. The agreement to open five points on the Line of Control (LoC) in order to provide relief and medical assistance to quake victims was widely acclaimed in J and K as a genuine humanitarian gesture by the two countries. "It is a good step" said Hurriyat

leader Mirwaiz Umar Farooq. Ms. Mehbooba Mufti, Chairperson of the ruling People's Democratic Party said such steps were imperative for taking the process of restoration of peace and reconciliation forward. "I am very happy that it is happening. It was very much needed," she said adding "this is the beginning. We'll have to go a long way before the dream of oneness, harmony and affinity is translated into reality." On November 5, the Spokesperson Navtej Sarna told a media briefing that the necessary work to operationalise the five points was under way. He said that the crossing point at Chakan da Bagh (Poonch) would be operationalised on November 7, at Kaman (Uri) on November 9 and Tithwal (Tangdhar) on November 10, 2005. He clarified that due to non-availability or damage to infrastructure at the above crossing points, crossing would be permitted on foot.

4. Samarjit Ghosh., loc. cit.
5. Stephen P. Cohen, Draft case study "The Compound Crisis of 2002" in *South Asia Amid Crisis,* The Brookings Institution, p. 31.
6. K.S. Manjunath., loc. cit.
7. The Pakistan Ministry of Foreign Affairs mentioned it in its official brief in 2005. See http:// www.mofa.gov.pk/Pages/Brief.htm.
8. For example, American experts on South Asia like Selig Harrison and Teresita Schaffer. Kofi Anan said he was 'very pleased and encouraged'. Richard Boucher said it was 'constructive to relinquish the demand for a referendum to the status of Kashmir'. *BBC*, December 19, 2003, available at http://news.bbc.co.uk.
9. B. Raman, "Counter-Terrorism and Appeasement", *South Asia Analysis Group,* Paper no. 3365, 20 August 2009. Retrieved from: http://www.southasiaanalysis.org/papers34/paper3365.html.
10. Ashok K. Behuria, "Pakistan's Approach to Kashmir since the Lahore Agreement: Is There Any Change?" *Strategic Analysis,* Routledge UK, p. 441.
11. Musharraf, quoted in the *Daily Times*, October 26, 2004.
12. Ashok K. Behuria, op. cit., p. 442.
13. Reported in *The Dawn,* November 28, 2005.
14. Reported in *The Dawn*, November 29, 2005.

15. Musharraf's December 2006 proposal for demilitarisation and autonomy was debated widely and the Pakistani media isolated the options for review and discussion as demilitarisation, autonomy/self-governance, joint control/shared sovereignty, sovereign Kashmir with no international personality, readjustment of territory and free trade zone, and open border.
16. See reports on General Musharraf's address in a conference titled "Voices from Asia: Towards a Process of Cooperation and Security", in *Tribune*, February 16, 2007, at http:// www. tribuneindia.com/2007/20070216/world.htm.
17. Steve Coll, "The Back Channel", *The New Yorker*, March 2, 2009.
18. *Ibid.*
19. Praveen Swami, "Kashmir deal was almost done", *The Hindu*, 4th January 2014.
20. "PM Meets JKLF Leaders", *Epilogue*, Jammu, 2007, p. 120.
21. *The Hindu,* May 4, 2006.
22. Praveen Swami, "Bits of Consensus", *Frontline*, Vol. 24, No. 9, May 5-18, 2007, p. 25.
23. Mridusmita Borah, "Third Round Table Conference on Kashmir: Is there a Consensus?" *Institute of Peace and Conflict Studies*, New Delhi, # 2292, 16 May, 2007. Retrieved from: http:// www.ipcs.org/article/jammu-kashmir/third-round-table-conference-on-kashmir-is-there-a-consensus-2292.html.
24. The *Times of India*, January 25, 2008.
25. Ashok K. Behuria, op. cit., p. 443.
26. Ashutosh Misra, "An audit of the India-Pakistan peace process", *Australian Journal of International Affairs*, Vol. 61, No. 4, December 2007, p. 513.
27. *Ibid.*
28. Mani Shankar Aiyar, "India-Pakistan: Retrospect and Prospect", *Wilhelm Von Pochhammer Memorial Lecture*, New Delhi, 12th January 2011.
29. Samina Ahmad and VarunSahni, "Freezing the Fighting: Military Disengagement on Siachen Glacier," *Cooperative Monitoring*

Center Occasional Papers (Sandia National Laboratories, Albuquerque) 1998, p. 21.

30. Ashutosh Misra., loc. cit.
31. *Ibid.*
32. A day earlier on May 26 the Army Chief, General J.J. Singh said that India "wants that the 110 k.m. long actual ground position line on the Siachen glacier should be authenticated by Pakistan." Stating the Indian position, General Singh said that the country's interests "will be served only when the AGPL is authenticated". He said the country's basic position was that the present AGPL between NJ 9842 to upper Saltoro ridge should be authenticated as "it will safeguard the country's interests in the future". The army chief added that the Army had given the plans and feedback to the government on the issue. The official sources reiterated this position on the eve of External Affairs Minister's visit to Islamabad in October. It was stated that redeployment of Indian and Pakistani troops in the Siachen would be possible provided the two sides agreed on the current actual ground position. It was further stated that the two countries would have to arrive at an understanding on what would be done with the area where the troops were currently deployed. Media quoted official sources to say that India favoured plotting the further course of the Line of Control which stops at Point NJ9842. President Musharraf during his visit to New Delhi in April had agreed that there should be some form of verification of the actual ground positions in Siachen.
33. Ashutosh Misra., loc. cit.
34. Gurmeet Kanwal, "Does Siachen have Major Strategic Significance?" *Asian Tribune*, May 22, 2007.
35. "Siachen Conflict", *Wikipedia, the free encyclopedia.*
36. Sajad Padder, "The Composite Dialogue between India and Pakistan: Structure, Process and Agency", *Heidelberg Papers in South Asian and Comparative Politics,* Working Paper No. 65, February 2012, p. 7.37. Ashutosh Misra, *op. cit.*, p. 519.
38. *Ibid.*

39. *Ibid.*
40. Mallika Joseph, "Delhi Round of Indo-Pak Talks – II: Tulbul Navigation Project/Wullar Barrage", *Islamabad Policy Research Institute* (IPRI), November 21, 1998.
41. See Joint Statement on Indo-Pak Water Resources Secretary level talks on Wullar Barrage/Tulbul Navigation Project, 31 August, 2007.<http://pib.nic.in/newsite/erelease.aspx?relid=30782>.
42. Ashutosh Misra, op. cit., p. 514.
43. Muralidhar Reddy, "India, Pakistan seek to resolve dispute over coastal strip off Gujarat coast", *The Hindu,* May 29, 2005.
44. *Ashutosh Misra,* op. cit., pp. 514-15.
45. *Ibid.*
46. *Ibid.*
47. Sameer Suryakant Patil, "Indo-Pak Composite Dialogue: An Update", *Institute of Peace and Conflict Studies* (IPCS), Special Report, No. 53, June 2008, p. 6.
48. *Ibid.*
49. *Ibid.*
50. Javed Mahmood, Shafi Baloch, "UN keeps mum on Sir Creek dispute", *The Nation*, Pakistan, September 7, 2009.
51. Ashutosh Misra, op. cit. p. 515.
52. Ministry of External Affairs, Government of India, 2005, 'Joint Press Statement at the End of Home Secretary Level Talks between India and Pakistan on Terrorism and Drug Trafficking', New Delhi, 30 August <http://meaindia.nic.in>.
53. Joint Statement, Third Round of Pakistan-India Interior/Home Secretary Talks on Terrorism and Drugs Trafficking, Islamabad, 31 May 2006, at <http://meaindia.nic.in>.
54. Joint Statement, India-Pakistan in Havana, Cuba, 16 September 2006, at <http://meaindia.nic.in>.
55. Shabana Fayyaz, "Indo-Pak Joint Anti-Terrorism Mechanism: Perspectives from Pakistan", *Institute of Peace and Conflict Studies (IPCS),* Issue Brief 126, September 2009, p. 1.
56. *Ibid.*, p. 2.

57. Joint Press Statement, Pakistan-India Interior/Home Secretary-Level Talks on Terrorism and Drugs Trafficking, Ministry of Foreign Affairs, Pakistan, July 4, 2007, at <http://www.mofa.gov.pk>.
58. *Ibid.*
59. Joint Statement issued at the end of the Home/Interior Secretary level talks between India and Pakistan in Islamabad on 25-26 November 2008, Ministry of External Affairs, New Delhi, November 26, 2008.
60. Ishtiaq Ahmed, "India-Pakistan Relations: Post-Mumbai Terrorist Attacks", *Institute of South Asian Studies* (ISAS), National University of Singapore (NUS), Insights No. 89, January 7, 2010, p. 1.
61. Ranjit Singh Ghuman, Davinder Kumar Madaan, "India-Pakistan Trade Co-operation and SAARC", *Peace and Democracy in South Asia*, Vol. 2, No. 1 and 2, 2006, p. 74.
62. Kanti P. Bajpai et al., *Brasstacks and Beyond: Perception and Management of Crisis in South Asia,* Manohar, New Delhi, 1995, pp. 9-10.
63. *The Hindu,* April 11, 1999.
64. Ashutosh Misra, *op. cit*., p. 520.
65. K.S. Manjunath, Seema Sridhar and Beryl Anand, "Indo-Pak Composite Dialogue 2004-05: A Profile", *Institute of Peace and Conflict Studies (IPCS),* New Delhi, Special Report 12, February, 2006. Retrieved from: http://www.ipcs.org/pdf_file/issue/1372586579IPCS-Special-Report-12.pdf.
66. Joint Statement, Third Round of Pakistan-India Talks on Economic and Commercial cooperation, Islamabad, 29 March, 2006, at http://meaindia.nic.in/jshome.htm.
67. Joint Statement on the Fourth Round of India Pakistan talks on Economic and Commercial Cooperation, New Delhi, August 1 2007, at <http://indembkwt.org/press/aug0107.htm>.
68. Joint Statement on the Fourth Round of India-Pakistan talks on Economic and Commercial Cooperation, New Delhi; August 1, 2007, at <http://indembkwt.org/press/aug0107.htm>.

69. Samarjit Ghosh, "Indo-Pak Composite Dialogue—2008: A Review", *Institute of Peace and Conflict Studies* (IPCS), New Delhi, Special Report 65, February 2009, p. 5.
70. *Ibid.*
71. 50 Years of Pakistan in Statistics, and Ministry of Commerce, Government of Pakistan.
72. Sandeep Dikshit, "Zardari for emulating India-China model for better ties", *The Hindu,* April 9, 2012.
73. C. Raja Mohan, "After Attari", *The Indian Express,* April 16, 2012.
74. Smruti S. Pattanaik and ArpitaAnant, "Cross-LoC Confidence Building Measures between India and Pakistan: A Giant Leap or a Small Step towards Peace?, *Institute of Defence Studies and Analyses, New Delhi*, Issue Brief, February 12, 2010, p. 21.
75. Joint Statement following meeting between the Minister of External Affairs of India and Minister of Foreign Affairs of Pakistan, July 27, 2011, Retrieved from: www.mea.gov.in
76. *The Hindu*, September 9, 2004.
77. *Dawn,* May 15, 2005.
78. Joint Press Statement on 'India-Pakistan Discussion on Promotion of Friendly Exchanges in Various Fields', New Delhi, 4th August 2004, at <http://meaindia.nic.in/declarestatement /2004/08/904js01.htm>.
79. Ashutosh Misra, *op. cit.*, p. 521.
80. *Ibid.*
81. *Ibid.*
82. *Ibid.*
83. *Ibid.*

4

Challenges to the Composite Dialogue Process

A peace process is a time consuming exercise based on the mutual desire of finding a peaceful solution to a conflict. Reciprocity is the most important element of any peace process. It should largely be indigenous in nature, with possible external assistance if desired by the parties concerned. A peace process cannot be launched, unless some basic requirements are met. Although these requirements might differ from case to case yet they can be used without major modifications. Some of the essential requirements of a peace process are:[1]

- Willingness of the parties concerned to initiate the process of negotiations.
- Clear intentions of the leaders involved in a peace process.
- Application of patience and persistence.
- Consideration of the time factor.
- Political will to sustain the process of negotiations.
- Reduction of mutual mistrust, suspicion, and paranoia.
- Creating conducive environment for negotiations.
- Identification of critical issues.
- Moving from less contentious to critical issues.
- Developing points of understanding.

- Striving for a win-win situation.
- Taking public opinion into confidence during the process of negotiations.
- Utilising the services of a mediator, if necessary.
- Learning lessons from relevant cases, if necessary.
- Highlighting the positive aspects of negotiations and learning from past failures in negotiations.
- Engaging the media in building an environment of mutual confidence and trust.
- Cessation of propaganda warfare against the adversary.
- Controlling border tensions.
- Maintaining better lines of communication between the policy-makers of the parties concerned.

Factors Affecting the Peace Process

There are a number of factors which play a very important role in the success of any peace process.

- Strong yearning for peace both at the governmental and public level.
- A peace process cannot be initiated unless the time is ripe for it.
- External involvement and encouragement in case of a stalemate.
- Patience because the peace process by nature is time consuming; if patience is missing, then incidents like an accident, terror attack can derail the whole process.
- The process is simply a mechanism for achieving the content; if the focus is allowed to shift away from the content it could distort priorities and have a negative impact on the peace process as a whole.[2]

A successful peace process should address the concerns of both or all parties regardless of their strength. If one side monopolises the agenda, the concerns of the weaker party are ignored and this adversely affects the peace process. To make or maintain peace, parties have to co-operate mutually. However, there are certain factors that may stop two adversaries from establishing peace between them. For instance, if the peace making effort lacks public support then these efforts can be taken as a sign of weakness. Another challenge is that in the absence of the institutionalisation of peace, the leadership of the involved parties will remain doubtful of the each other's intentions and commitment to the process. Another important issue is what both sides are getting out of the process and how the gains are used. If a certain party is getting more than the other, the chances of the other party to back off will increase because it will start thinking that it will be left nowhere if the other side, after getting whatever it wants, defects and that use the gain against it in any future confrontation.

The India-Pakistan Composite Dialogue is the most positive development in recent times. It arose out of, and after, the serious negativity and downturn that occurred in India-Pakistan relations from the late 1990s until late 2003. During this period, three major events occurred in India-Pakistan relations. First, both nations confirmed their respective nuclear capabilities via nuclear tests in 1998.[3] Second, they engaged in a localised conventional conflict — some call it a war as there were over 1,000 deaths — in the Kargil area of the disputed former princely state of Jammu and Kashmir in 1999. Third, they mobilised forces for apparent war in late 2001-early 2002 after India's strong response to the attack on its parliament on 13th December 2001 that New Delhi alleged involved terrorists sponsored by Pakistan.[4] Encouraged by strong external diplomacy, cooler heads in New Delhi and Islamabad ultimately and thankfully prevailed. Thereafter, as a result of an agreement between Prime Minister Atal Behari Vajpayee and General Pervez Musharraf, the India-Pakistan Composite Dialogue was revived in 2004. As India sees it, the dialogue is built on 'three pillars'—the absence of violence, including Pakistan not permitting terrorism against India in any manner from its territory, finding peaceful solutions to all outstanding issues including Jammu and Kashmir and building a cooperative relationship between India and Pakistan.[5] For Pakistan, the overall objective has been to construct a multi-faceted good neighbourly relationship with India and build durable peace in the region.[6] Since 2004, four rounds of serious discussions have taken place between Indian and Pakistani officials on eight issues in order to try and resolve all of their outstanding and contentious issues to the satisfaction of both sides.[7] This Composite Dialogue Process continues, even though the peace process has been under strain in recent months.[8] The eight issues being discussed in the dialogue are: peace and security, including confidence-building measures (CBMs); Jammu and Kashmir; Siachen Glacier; the Wullar Barrage/Tulbul Navigation project; Sir Creek; terrorism and drug trafficking; economic and commercial cooperation; and, the promotion of friendly exchanges. In the four rounds so far concluded, there have not been any significant or groundbreaking agreements on any of the big issues. However, there have been a number of important bilateral achievements, including MoUs and agreements on various issues, a reaffirmation of a determination not to let terrorism impede the peace process and progress on promoting a stable environment of peace and security including CBMs.[9] At the conclusion of the fourth round, which was delayed due to political events in Pakistan, dates for the fifth round of the Composite Dialogue were announced for July 2008. Prime Minister Manmohan Singh and President Asif Zardari re-affirmed that this dialogue should proceed in their joint press statement made on September 25, 2008 when they met at the United Nations General Assembly.[10] The fact that this dialogue has continued despite a temporary downturn in bilateral relations, including some firing across the Line of Control (LoC) and a very negative statement by India's National Security Adviser, M.K. Narayanan, after the bombing of the Indian embassy in Kabul, is a positive development.[11] Anything that keeps India and Pakistan engaged is a good thing.

The fifth round of the Composite Dialogue began in July 2008.[12] Speaking before the start of this round, Pakistan's Foreign Minister, Makhdoom Shah Mehmood Qureshi believed that the early resolution of the Siachen Glacier and Sir Creek issues was 'doable', provided that there was the political will for their expeditious resolution. These resolutions then would enable India and Pakistan to move speedily in other areas.[13] India's External Affairs Minister Pranab Mukherjee was more sanguine. He applauded the resurgence of democracy and popular participation in Pakistan as a 'positive factor' for the India-Pakistan relationship. However, he also saw the need to deepen the levels of cooperation in the economic and commercial fields and hoped for further concrete achievements to pave the way for a qualitative transformation of our bilateral relations.[14]

The statements above by Mr. Qureshi and Mr. Mukherjee suggest that India and Pakistan have different approaches to the Composite

Dialogue. For Pakistan, its desire appears to be to get India to agree as soon as possible to resolutions to some of the serious issues that have bedeviled the India-Pakistan relationship. But it also reflects Islamabad's desire and need to achieve something concrete, given the significant compromise that Pakistan made by renouncing its long-held stance to resolve the 'unfinished business of partition', the Kashmir dispute, as a prerequisite to entering into a more involved and complex relationship with India. For India, the idea seems to be to 'hasten slowly' and build up strong economic links. This, arguably, has always been India's stance, although New Delhi also has compromised by agreeing to actually discuss the Kashmir dispute in a meaningful way as part of the India-Pakistan Composite Dialogue. As late as October 2003, Prime Minister Vajpayee was still insisting that the issue was not about how to resolve this territorial dispute but about when Pakistan would vacate those parts of Jammu and Kashmir that it occupied.[15]

The respective stands of India and Pakistan on the Composite Dialogue also reflect their differing strategic positions. Pakistan needs and wants, to resolve some of the issues in the Composite Dialogue fairly quickly, both to satisfy its population that typically is suspicious or fearful of India and also to enhance its generally inferior strategic or diplomatic position in relation to India. In terms of the eight items in the Composite Dialogue, Pakistan is in a lesser or weaker position on five of them. It is in the inferior territorial position in Jammu and Kashmir with no access to the coveted Kashmir Valley. It is also in the downstream position on the water issue of the Wullar Barrage/Tulbul Navigation project and generally on all of the rivers in the Indus Waters Treaty. Similarly, its forces are apparently in the downhill or tactically-inferior position on the Siachen Glacier (although they are in the superior position in terms of accessing the glacier).[16] It has also frequently been on the 'back foot' on the issue of terrorism and alleged Pakistan-inspired terrorist attacks in, or against, India and to a lesser extent, on drug trafficking, with significant amounts of drugs being smuggled from Afghanistan through Pakistan to foreign destinations, including India. Since Islamabad has not yet reciprocated the 'Most Favoured Nation' status to India, that is the basis for engaging in effective two-way trade, so it is under some obligation on the issue of economic and commercial cooperation. For the other three issues i.e., peace and security including CBMs, Sir Creek, and the promotion of friendly exchanges, both nations appear to be at parity.

Conversely, India is the status quo power, with seemingly little incentive or desires to resolve many of the important India-Pakistan disagreements. India is in the superior strategic or diplomatic position on many of these issues. These include: in Jammu and Kashmir, where India has what it and Pakistan both want: the Kashmir Valley; waters for irrigation and hydro-electricity that flow through disputed Jammu and Kashmir and on to Pakistan, with India able to control and manipulate many of these important flows; the high tactical positions on Siachen Glacier (positions the Indian military is very reluctant to forego); the stronger, more dynamic and more resilient economy (which Pakistan might obtain benefit from being involved with); and, the moral 'high ground' on terrorism. Unlike Islamabad, New Delhi does not appear to feel any need to obtain quick solutions on any of the eight items in the Composite Dialogue. Indeed, with Pervez Musharraf's political demise, New Delhi might well have missed a genuine opportunity to resolve the Kashmir dispute on terms that may have been reasonably acceptable to it — although much more negotiation and clarification was needed to determine whether Musharraf's 'out of the box' four-point solution in December, 2006 applied to all of Jammu and Kashmir.[17] One area outside the dialogue where Pakistan potentially is strong would be the Iran-Pakistan-India (IPI) gas pipeline, via Baluchistan. However, India also appears to be in no rush to conclude this agreement, partly because it has been finalising its 123 Agreement with the United States. The US also apparently has been pressuring India to move away from Iran, including by not supporting IPI gas pipeline agreement.

The India-Pakistan Composite Dialogue Process is being challenged by several entrenched factors as follows:

The First Entrenched Factor: Leadership

Historically, several entrenched factors have impacted on the India-Pakistan 'peace process' and limited, or prevented, both nations from concluding significant and meaningful agreements on contentious bilateral issues, particularly the Kashmir dispute. The first factor is the need for strong, popular, conciliatory and decisive leadership concurrently in both nations that can make appropriate agreements on divisive issues. Both India and Pakistan have had strong and decisive leaders at times. They also have had popular and conciliatory leaders at times. However, neither nation has had leaders with all of these four qualities at any one time — and at the same time. Hence, while the Indian leaders such as Jawaharlal Nehru, Indira Gandhi or Rajiv Gandhi were strong and popular, they generally were not sufficiently conciliatory and decisive in relation to Pakistan, especially over the contentious issue of Jammu and Kashmir. Later leaders such as Atal Behari Vajpayee or Manmohan Singh may have been relatively more conciliatory than the Nehru-Gandhi's in wanting to advance India-Pakistan relations, but they have lacked the political strength and popularity to enable them to be decisive and to deliver solutions. Pakistan has suffered from the same problem. Many of its leaders have been strong and decisive, but they have not been sufficiently conciliatory and, particularly, they have lacked popular support, especially military leaders such as Ayub Khan or Zia-ul-Haq. Zulfikar Ali Bhutto was a strong and popular politician, but his nation's position on Jammu and Kashmir was weak and compromised due to the effects of the 1971 India-Pakistan war. Nawaz Sharif was in a strong and popular political position in 1997-1999 but his Indian counterpart, Atal Behari Vajpayee, was not. A similar situation applied to the Pervez Musharraf-Manmohan Singh relationship. Musharraf was strong but increasingly unpopular, while Singh was popular but increasingly politically weak.

History shows, therefore, that India and Pakistan generally have not been able to overcome many of their major issues because they have lacked leaders with sufficient amounts of all of the four above-mentioned characteristics concurrently. There have been some India-Pakistan agreements achieved, such as the Indus Waters Treaty of 1960, 'the only agreement that has been faithfully implemented and upheld by both India and Pakistan'[18] and the Rann of Kutch arbitration of 1968. Interestingly, the completion of these has involved third party assistance. The appearance or production of appropriate leadership that might be willing and able to solve the Kashmir dispute is out of the hands of the people of India and Pakistan. Such suitable conciliatory leadership will only appear as a result of a period of good luck in both nations. That is, it will be arbitrary and purely fortuitous. One way that weaker, less decisive leadership could be encouraged or compelled to act would be by an active, forceful and conciliatory democratic polity that strongly wanted to see India-Pakistan relations improve and normalise.

The Second Entrenched Factor: Public Opinion

The preservation of peace depends upon the maintenance of a state of public opinion favourable to peace. Equally, the successful conduct of a war depends upon the creation of a state of public opinion characterised by hatred and enmity towards other nations. Public opinion is an aggregate of the individual views, attitudes and beliefs about a particular topic or event, expressed by a significant proportion of a community or population. The American political scientist V.O. Key defines public opinion as "opinions held by private persons which governments find it prudent to heed." Political scientists and some historians have tended to emphasise the role of public opinion in government and politics, paying particular attention to its influence on the development of government policy. Indeed, some political scientists have regarded public opinion as equivalent to the national will.

Public opinion plays a significant role in Indo-Pak relations. Keeping in view the long history of hostile relations between the two countries only a favourable public opinion could unite them. Public opinion is formed through a complex process. In this information age, mass media plays an important role in shaping the public opinion. It includes newspapers, radio, television, and the internet. Since the days of partition of India in 1947 media has not played any constructive role in bridging the trust deficit between the two countries. Shortly after signing of the Nehru-Liaquat pact in 1950, editors and senior journalists of both countries met in New Delhi in May 1950. They took note of the violence caused by inaccurate analysis and misperceptions generated by the content of the radio broadcasts and reports published and newspapers and journals. They deeply regretted the consequences of lapses and resolved to prevent recurrence in the future. But this good resolve of May, 1950 soon got dissolved.[19]

It is generally found that the young generations of both India and Pakistan, quite unawares of the common past, have negative perceptions of one another. This is evident from the fact that a simple statement of peace and harmony by the political leaders of either country invites hatred and animosity on social networking sites like facebook, twitter etc. India and Pakistan have several unresolved disputes like Kashmir, Siachen, Sir Creek, Tulbul Navigation Project etc. Kashmir has been a thorny issue right from 1947. The two countries have fought two major wars over Kashmir. Kashmir spews-out jingoism even from the well-educated people. During the 2010, Kashmir unrest, Arundhati Roy had to delete her facebook page following abuses over her stance on Kashmir issue. During a workshop at Amritsar (April, 2013) Pandit-ji, a participant from Haryana denounced us by saying: "*tum doodh maangoge hum kheer denge…tum Kashmir mangoge hum cheer denge*". It seems the argumentative Indian is turning angry with every passing day.

From 2004 to 2008 the India-Pakistan composite dialogue process gained momentum. It resulted in a number of Confidence Building Measures. A cease-fire was established along the LoC since November 2003. The air and road connectivity improved between the two countries. There were frequent exchanges of students, academics, doctors, artists, sportsmen and parliamentarians. Even agreements on few important issues like Siachen and Sir Creek seemed within reach. The back channel was also active on Kashmir during this period. Indian Prime Minister Dr Manmohan Singh, in a significant revelation, for the first time, publicly acknowledged that secret envoys from the two countries had almost arrived at an agreed resolution to end the conflict in Kashmir. "At one time it appeared an important breakthrough was in sight. However, in Pakistan, General Pervez Musharraf had to make way for a different set of leaders. I think that led to the process not moving properly. However, I still believe that good relations between India and Pakistan are possible."[20] Another event that finally halted the dialogue process was the November 26, 2008 Mumbai terror attacks. Just an hour before the attackers fired the first shot, the Indian and Pakistani Foreign Ministers were holding a press conference in New Delhi. The tension between the two countries at the time was over the Indian cricket team's hesitation to go play a series in Pakistan after the Marriott hotel bombing in Islamabad. Coincidentally, India's Home Secretary was in Islamabad, where the two countries had issued a comprehensive Joint Statement on fighting Terror and Drug

Trafficking. India and Pakistan had agreed to 'fast-track' the fifth round of the Composite Dialogue. Hours later, all dialogue was suspended, and history was written once again by the terrorist's gun. Television channels flooded the spot of attacks with live coverage. In order to improve their Television Rating Points media houses are abuzz with anchors playing hand in hand with former military generals. The buck actually stops nowhere. For these reasons, Prof Pratap Bhanu Mehta, a renowned Indian Political Scientist, views such TV debates as no more than entertainment shows.

What can be done to repair this impaired public opinion? Mere elite meetings like Pugwash or Chaophraya Conferences are of little help. Such meetings invite academics, media persons, politicians and former military officials to discuss issues in an informal way. But over the years even in these meetings hardly any real consensus is emerging on important issues. One NGO which has done some commendable work and is accessible to all is the Pakistan-India People's Forum for Peace and Democracy. Some concrete steps should be taken to positively mould the perceptions of people for longtime peace and prosperity in the region.

As the first step, the school textbooks in both countries need to be reframed. The textbooks in India and Pakistan present divergent views on historical events. In this direction, the History Project is a good beginning. It was founded by three young Pakistanis: Qasim Aslam, Ayyaz Ahmad and Zoya Siddiqui. The History Project, comprising excerpts from three Indian textbooks and nine Pakistani textbooks, provides students an illuminating comparison of the ways that key historical events—leading up to partition—are taught in schools in both countries.

Let us take the example of Kashmir:

History textbook in India: In 1947, when Hari Singh, the ruler of Kashmir, opted to stay independent, Pakistani armed intruders from Pakistan attacked Kashmir. Hari Singh then signed an agreement to join India, and the Indian army was sent in to defend Kashmir.

History textbook in Pakistan: Hari Singh started a brutal campaign to drive out Muslims from Kashmir. Over 200,000 people in the princely state, supported by the tribesmen of the Northwest Frontier Province, were successful in liberating a large area of Kashmir from the Maharaja's control. So, Hari Singh was forced to turn to India for help and in return acceded to India.[21]

As a result, two groups of children are growing up with different ideas about a shared past. According to a report by the US Commission on International Religious Freedom, text books in Pakistani schools also foster prejudice and intolerance of Hindus and other religious minorities. Hindus are repeatedly described as extremists and eternal enemies of Islam whose culture and society is based on injustice and cruelty.[22] A generation feed on such biases is found to be intolerant and vulnerable to extremism.

Secondly, media in both countries needs to be socialised in peace building. Even the former President of India A.P.J. Abdul Kalam observed that we only read about death, sickness, terrorism and crime. Why are we so negative…? A good example is set by the two leading media houses, The Jang Group in Pakistan and The Times of India. They have jointly launched a peace campaign, "*Aman Ki-Asha*" in 2010. Commenting on the achievements of Aman Ki Asha, Beena Sarwar, a Pakistani writer opines, "For millions of Indians and Pakistanis, *Aman Ki-Asha* is just that—a shared 'hope for peace' between our two countries. Despite falsehoods circulated by detractors targeting this peace initiative in all kinds of underhand ways since its launch on January 1, 2010, it has stayed the course, and continued to urge both governments to do so. In the process, *Aman Ki-Asha* has provided a platform and a way forward for aspirations of peace between India and Pakistan."[23]

Thirdly, trade is a key to bring peace and prosperity in the region and our leaders should accept this fact and work on it. India and China have successfully moved on the trade front but the Indo-Pak trade is marred due to political tensions. Since 2004, trade between India and Pakistan has increased from $ 500 million to $ 2.5 billion in 2013. The actual potential of trade is estimated to be more than $ 10 billion annually. Estimates from gravity models suggest that trade between the two countries could reach to $ 20 billion.[24] On positive development in recent years was the start of the cross LoC trade between Srinagar-Muzaffarabad and Pooch-Rawalakot in Jammu and Kashmir in year 2008. To begin with it was believed to be an important confidence building measure. Slowly this optimism has faded away. The governments of India and Pakistan have adopted uncompromising attitudes towards cross LoC trade. It is still a medieval type barter trade with only 21 items allowed for exchanged. The partition of India has disrupted many other regional trade routes as well. There is a strong demand for opening up the Hussainiwala border in Punjab.[25] Apart from promoting economic activity the opening of this border would also help in further strengthening the socio-cultural ties amongst the people of both the countries. Revealing his vision of India-Pakistan ties in 2007 Indian Prime Minister Dr Manmohan Singh famously said that I am looking for a day when "one can have breakfast in Amritsar, lunch in Lahore and dinner in Kabul." But unfortunately Dr Singh, during his two stints as Prime Minister, never visited Pakistan while his predecessor Mr Vajpayee has made two visits.

Fourthly, sports and cultural exchanges should not be kept hostage to political relations. Cricket has helped in bridging the divide, allowing the fans from both sides to travel to the other country to watch the match and enjoy mutual hospitality. Such exchanges have shaped people's perceptions positively in both countries towards each other. In 1987, General Zia-ul Haq flew to Jaipur, in India, to watch a cricket match. General Musharraf followed suit almost two decades later, coming to watch an India-Pakistan match in New Delhi during his state visit in April, 2005. Pakistani Prime Minister Mr Yousuf Raza Gilani also visited Mohali in 2011 to watch the cricket World Cup semifinal between India and Pakistan with his Indian counterpart Dr Manmohan Singh. Sport transcends borders. But since the 2008 Mumbai attacks, cricket and other sports exchanged were stopped. The worst case was when India returned Pakistani hockey players back without allowing them to play even a single match in the Hockey India League, 2013. By succumbing to the pressure of Shiv Sena, the government of India has set a wrong precedent. Demands have echoed later to ban Sri Lankan cricket players from playing in the Indian Premier League.

Lastly, Bollywood and Lollywood could turn out to be good conduits for peace. It is quite unnatural to ban the movies from either side. The Indian film industry's perception of Pakistan has always been dependent on the mood of the nation and government policies. But now, filmmakers keep in mind the mood of the market as well as Pakistan is emerging as a huge market for Bollywood films. When recently the ban on Bollywood movies was lifted in Pakistan, the Chennai Express could make Rs 40 million a week and that too from the city of Karachi only.

Public opinion acts as a powerful restraint against war. Governments are wary of going to war because they expect to pay an electoral penalty for ghting even successful wars. The rules of the game change once public opinion is nurtured for war. History proves that such a policy is short lived. President Lyndon Johnson and President George W. Bush enjoyed considerable public support to intervene in Vietnam and Iraq respectively. But the public support for war sharply declined and forced the withdrawal of troops from both places. India and Pakistan need to change for good.

The Third Entrenched Factor: The Trust Deficit

The biggest problem and a spoiling factor for the peace process from the very beginning was the trust deficit between the two sides. This poses actual problems in resolving some specific issues. The litmus test is the Siachen Glacier. The 'trust deficit' is not just a factor that affects the people of one nation only. Based on personal experience, it can be found in copious quantities among people on both sides of the India-Pakistan border.[26] The trust deficit is actually a deep and abiding mutual mistrust of each other based on a strong and residual sense of having been aggrieved by actions perpetrated by the other nation.[27] The fact that the people of both nations have had almost nothing to do with one another since 1947 has only helped this phenomenon to grow.

The 'trust deficit' between the Indians and the Pakistanis traces its origins back to issues in 1947. These included: the Radcliffe Award and Lord Mountbatten's alleged nefarious part in this award, by which some Pakistanis believe that Pakistan was cheated out of Muslim-majority Gurdaspur District, thereby giving India a land route to Jammu and Kashmir; to Maharaja Hari Singh's accession to India on 26th October, 1947, which the Pakistan Government believed was obtained by India by means of 'fraud and violence';[28] to the invasion of Kashmir province by Pukhtoon tribesmen on 22nd October, 1947, which India alleges was supported, if not instigated, by Pakistan (but which resulted in Hari Singh's accession to India).[29] For India, mistrust of Pakistan was reinforced by events in 1965. For Pakistan, mistrust of India was furthered by the nefarious part that New Delhi played in the Bengali insurgency and the dismemberment of Pakistan in 1971. For India, mistrust was again fuelled by alleged 'foreign hand' involvement in many of its more recent internal insurgencies, such as with disenchanted Sikhs in the 1980s and with Pakistan-sponsored anti-Indian militants in the Kashmir Valley since 1989. Conversely, Pakistan has seen, and continues to see, 'foreign hand' involvement in its problems in Baluchistan, and recently in the Federally-Administered Tribal Areas (FATA) of the North-West Frontier Province.[31] For Pakistan, it was heightened by Indian military activities like 'Operation Brasstacks', when the Indian military massively and provocatively mobilised near the Pakistan border in 1986-1987 in a purported exercise, by India's development of a military nuclear capability, and more recently, by India's attempts to acquire a 'blue water' naval capability.[32] These Indian actions confirm the belief held by some Pakistanis that India does not accept Pakistan's existence and that it wants to re-integrate Pakistan. This unrealistic belief is a very telling aspect of the entire India-Pakistan 'trust deficit' regime. It limits Pakistan's ability to engage fully with, and to benefit fully from its relations with India.

The Fourth Entrenched Factor: Terrorism

The fourth entrenched factor that has hindered the smooth running of Composite Dialogue process is the issue of terrorism. The thaw in India-Pakistan relations began in April, 2003 and resulted in ceasefire on the LoC on 26th November, 2003. On 6th January 2004, at the end of the SAARC Summit in Islamabad, the two sides signed a joint statement that revived composite dialogue. The joint statement that formed the basis of composite dialogue between India and Pakistan, hinged on drawing a delicate balance between India's concern on terrorism and Pakistan's apprehension regarding the marginalisation of the Kashmir issue. The statement said: "the resumption of the composite dialogue will lead to peaceful settlement of all bilateral issues, including Jammu and Kashmir". Islamabad agreed that it "would not permit any territory under Pakistan's control to be used to support terrorism in any manner."[33] This implied a subtle linkage in the progress on the two issues.

Consequently, Kashmir and terrorism have dominated the composite dialogue that began in March, 2004. The experience of Composite Dialogue over the years indicates that India and Pakistan sharply differ regarding progress on Kashmir and terrorism. Pakistan feels that there has not been concrete progress on the resolution of Kashmir while it has done everything to address India's concern about 'cross-border terrorism'. Conversely, India feels that Pakistan has still not given up the *jihadi* option on Kashmir and questions its sincerity and commitment to curb cross-border terrorism. The joint statements issued at the end of each round of talks on the peace and security and Kashmir or the foreign secretaries review talks, show that both sides want to register the importance they attach to their respective concerns on Kashmir and terrorism. For instance in September, 2004, the joint statement at the end of the foreign secretaries review meeting underscored, 'carrying the process forward in an atmosphere free from terrorism and violence' and 'continue with the serious and sustained dialogue to find a peaceful negotiated final settlement' of the Kashmir dispute.[34] In October, 2005, the joint statement issued at the end of second round of talks reiterated that "possible options for a peaceful, negotiated settlement of the issue of Jammu and Kashmir should be explored in a sincere, purposeful and forward-looking manner." It also re-affirmed determination not to allow terrorism to impede the peace process.[35] The joint statement issued on 16th September, 2006, at the end of Musharraf Manmohan meeting, the leaders decided to continue the joint search for mutually acceptable options for a peaceful negotiated settlement of all issues between India and Pakistan, including the issue of Jammu and Kashmir in a sincere and purposeful manner. It emphasised the need to build on convergences and narrow down divergences. The leaders strongly condemned all acts of terrorism and agreed that terrorism is a scourge that needs to be effectively dealt with. They decided to put in place 'an India-Pakistan anti-terrorism institutional mechanism to identify and implement counter-terrorism initiatives and investigations.'[36]

The leadership on both sides has showed considerable political will and commitment to sustain the composite dialogue on Kashmir and terrorism. However, their statements from time to time have voiced sharp difference in their respective stances over improving situation in Kashmir and the resolution of the dispute. Indian leadership has continued to highlight the issue of 'cross-LoC infiltration' and terrorism and contended that it is directly linked with the reduction of troops from the Indian administered Kashmir. Hence, India has not agreed to CBMs that could normalise situation inside Kashmir such as extending ceasefire to the militants, announcing gradual reduction of troops, abrogating repressive laws such as Armed Forces Special Powers Act, etc. India has linked all these steps to the security situation in Kashmir. In contrast, Pakistani leadership continued to make efforts to keep Kashmir at the centre of the dialogue and emphasised on the Kashmir specific CBMs.[37]

Fig. Terror Attack on Taj Hotel in Mumbai on November 27, 2008.

On the night of the Mumbai terror attacks of November 26, 2008, just an hour before the attackers fired the first shot, the Indian and Pakistani Foreign Ministers were holding a press conference in New Delhi. The tension between the two countries at the time was over the Indian cricket team's hesitation to go play a series in Pakistan after the Marriott hotel bombing in Islamabad. Coincidentally, India's Home Secretary was in Islamabad, where the two countries had issued a comprehensive Joint Statement on fighting Terror and Drug Trafficking. India and Pakistan had agreed to 'fast-track' the fifth round of the Composite Dialogue.[38] Hours later all dialogue was suspended, and history was written once again by the terrorist's gun.

The Mumbai attacks of November, 2008 had led to the most prolonged suspension of talks since the year 2000. In May 2006, negotiators were close to a breakthrough on demilitarising the Siachen glacier, which Prime Minister Manmohan Singh had hoped to make a "mountain of peace."[39]

But first deadly attacks at the Congress party rally in Srinagar on the eve of the Prime Minister's roundtable conference, and another brutal attack on tourists, pushed Siachen talks to July, when the Foreign Secretaries were due to meet. In July 2006, just nine days before that meeting, the Mumbai train bombings left more than 200 dead and with them buried all talk of talks for months. Delhi suspended composite dialogue after Mumbai train blasts on 11th July, 2006 which was restored only when Pakistan agreed to the formation of an anti-terrorism institutional mechanism to address India's concerns on terrorism. A joint anti-terror panel was set up in this regard which had its first meeting in March 2007. Sharp differences have arisen in the very first meeting as Pakistan maintained that incidents inside Jammu and Kashmir would not come in the purview of the anti-terror panel while India insisted that it should cover all terror incidents whether they are in India or Kashmir. The working of the mechanism posed a huge challenge to both sides, as they tried to use it to their own advantage.

In 2007, revived talks made strides on the Wullar dispute. They had all but agreed on a settlement on Sir Creek when the Samjhauta blasts took place. Again and again, the dialogue was buffeted in a series of blasts, in Hyderabad, Jaipur, Ahmedabad, Bangalore and Delhi, where more than a hundred people were killed. In 2008, it was the bombing of the Indian Embassy in Kabul, and then the Mumbai attacks, that finally halted all talks. Through these brutalities, the composite dialogue has lurched from event to event, sustaining itself on the oxygen of meetings on the sidelines of international summits—Havana, Colombo, New York, L'Aguilla, Yekaterinburg and Sharm-el-Sheikh. In Jammu and Kashmir, the attack on Fazl Haq Qureshi in Srinagar and the *fidayeen* hotel siege at Lal Chowk have followed reports of dialogue being initiated between the Central government and separatists.

All these impending deadlines, coupled with the window of opportunity for talks in Kashmir, hasten the need for a new line of engagement between New Delhi and Islamabad—an engagement that understands that agencies that have unleashed terror attacks to derail the process in the past will shadow the next round too. Therefore, a process of "uninterrupted and uninterruptible dialogue" is the only way forward.[40]

Notes

1. RizwanZeb, "Peace Process: Spoilers and Indo-Pak Conflict", Pak Institute for Peace Studies (PIPS), Islamabad, Pakistan, September 29, 2009, pp. 2-3.
2. Ibid.
3. Christopher Snedden, "The India-Pakistan Peace Process: Stronger, but with some interference", *Institute of Regional Studies* (IRS), Seminar Papers, Islamabad, 20-21 Oct 2008.
4. While some consider the attack on the Indian parliament on 13 December 2001 to be the first terrorist attack after 9/11, the first such attack was actually on the Jammu and Kashmir Legislative Assembly, Srinagar, on 1 October 2001.
5. Briefing by Indian foreign secretary after India-Pakistan Foreign Secretary level talks, 21/07/2008', Indian Ministry of External Affairs, website, http://meaindia.nic.in/pressbriefing/2008/07/21pb 02.htm.
6. Address by the Foreign Minister of Pakistan at the International Conference on "Pakistan-India Peace Process: The Way Forward", 26 August 2008', Ministry of Foreign Affairs, Pakistan, website: http://www.mofa. gov. pk.
7. Institute of Strategic Studies, "India and Pakistan: Towards Greater Bilateral Stability", *Strategic Survey,* Vol. 104, No.1, May 2004, p. 232.
8. India-Pakistan Joint Press Statement issued after meeting of Indian Prime Minister Manmohan Singh with President of Pakistan Asif Ali Zardari in New York, 24 September 2008, Indian Ministry of External Affairs, "Joint Declarations and Statements", http:// meaindia. nic. in/
9. Joint Statement issued after Foreign Minister level Review of the Fourth Round of Composite Dialogue, Islamabad, 21 May 2008', Indian Ministry of External Affairs website, http://meaindia.nic.in/
10. India-Pakistan Joint Press Statement issued after meeting of the Prime Minister with the President of Pakistan in New York, 24 September 2008', Indian Ministry of External Affairs, "Joint Declarations and Statements", http://meaindia.nic.in/ Joint

Statement issued after Foreign Minister level Review of the Fourth Round of Composite Dialogue, Islamabad, 21 May 2008', Indian Ministry of External Affairs website, http://meaindia.nic.in/

11. Praveen Swami, "Fighting Pakistan's informal war", *The Hindu,* Jul 15, 2008.
12. Joint Press Conference of External Affairs Minister of India, Shri Pranab Mukherjee, and Foreign Minister of Pakistan, Makhdoom Shah Mehmood Qureshi, held at 1400 hours in Hyderabad House, New Delhi, 27/06/2008, Indian Ministry of External Affairs website, http://meaindia.nic.in/pressbriefing/ 2008/ 06/27pb01.htm
13. Address by the Foreign Minister of Pakistan at the International Conference on "Pakistan-India Peace Process: The Way Forward", 26 August 2008, Ministry of Foreign Affairs, Pakistan, website: http://www.mofa.gov.pk
14. Joint Press Conference of External Affairs Minister of India, and foreign Minister of Pakistan New Delhi, 27 June 2008.
15. Rajesh Ahuja, "Pak. must vacate occupied territory", *The Hindu,* Oct 19, 2003.
16. About the Siachen Glacier, <http://www.siachenglacier.com/>.
17. Prannoy Roy, "Pak ready to give up claim on Kashmir: Musharraf; *NDTV.com*, 5 December 2007, <http://www.ndtv.com>Musharraf's four points were: no change to the current boundaries; to make the borders and the LoC irrelevant; a staggered demilitarisation; and, autonomy or self-governance with a joint supervision mechanism. However, it was not clear if this autonomy and supervision related to all of Jammu and Kashmir, or to the Kashmir Valley, or to some other unspecified area. But, if India had been prepared to accept Musharraf's solution, then Pakistan was apparently prepared to give up its claim to Kashmir.
18. The Henry L. Stimson Center, "The Indus Waters Treaty", *Stimson,* <http://www.stimson.org/southasia/ ?sn=sa20020116300>.
19. Javed Jabbar, "Prospects of Improving Pakistan-India Relations through media", Background Paper, *PILDAT,* Islamabad, Pakistan, August 2012, p. 9.

20. 300. Praveen Swami, "Kashmir deal was almost done", *The Hindu,* 4 January 2014.
21. Swati Daftuar, "One story two sides", *The Hindu,* 14 September 2013. Also, QasimAslam, Ayyaz Ahmad and Zoya Siddiqui, "The History Project", *Seeds of Peace,* 2013.
22. Azhar Hussain and Ahmad Salim, "Connecting the Dots: Education and Religious Discrimination in Pakistan, United States Commission on International Religious Freedom, p. 43, November, 2011.
23. Beena Sarwar, "India, Pakistan and Aman Ki Asha", Retrieved from: http://amankiasha.com/detail_news.asp?id=1268.
24. Mohsin S. Khan, "India-Pakistan Trade: A Roadmap for Enhancing Economic Relations", *Peterson Institute for International Economics,* Policy Brief, p. 02, July 2009.
25. Dariya News, "CM for opening Hussainiwala border to step up economic activity in the Indian sub-continent", 19 December 2013. Retrieved from: http://www.diprpunjab.gov. in.
26. *Ibid.*
27. Christopher Snedden, "The India-Pakistan Peace Process: Overcoming the Trust Deficit", *Pakistan Security Research Unit (PSRU),* Brief Number 20, October 2, 2007, p. 5.
28. *Ibid.*
29. See White Paper on Jammu and Kashmir, [Delhi], Government of India, [1948].
30. Muhammad Ejaz Khan, "Musharraf sees foreign hand in Baluchistan unrest", *The News,* 5 August 2008, <http://www.thenews.com.pk/top_story_detail.asp?Id=16424>.
31. Spokesman Briefings of 26/06/2008', Ministry of Foreign Affairs, Pakistan, http://www.mofa.gov.pk/ Spokesperson/2008/June/Spokes_26_06_08.htm,Asked 'Is there any possibilities of involvement of the foreign hand in disturbances in FATA?' the Ministry of Foreign Affairs spokesperson responded that "There is presence of certain foreign element which is fanning trouble in our tribal areas. Expulsion of foreign elements from FATA is a priority task of the government." This may also refer to foreigners

other than the Indians in FATA, of course, although when referring to the 'foreign hand' in Pakistan, India invariably is implied.

32. 'Blue-water' (high seas) naval capability means that a fleet is able to operate on the "high seas."In this regard, the launch of the Arihant (nuclear-powered submarine) by the Indian Prime Minister in July 2009 is a significant milestone towards creating a robust sea based nuclear deterrent capability.
33. "Pakistan-India Joint statement", *Dawn,* Karachi, 7 January, 2004.
34. "Highlights of the Joint Statement", *The Times of India,* New Delhi, 9 September 2005.
35. "Text of Pakistan-India Joint Statement", *Daily Times,* Lahore, Pakistan, 5 October 2005.
36. India-Pakistan Joint Statement in Havana, Cuba, 16 September 2006, <http://meaindia.nic.in/jshome.htm>.
37. Interview with Aziz Ahmed Khan, the Ex. Pakistan's high commissioner to India, October 2009, Srinagar.
38. Suhasini Haidar, "India and Pakistan: deadlines for dialogue", *The Hindu,* January 12, 2010.
39. *Ibid.*
40. Mani Shankar Aiyar, "India-Pakistan: Retrospect and Prospect", *Wilhelm Von Pochhammer Memorial Lecture,* New Delhi, 12 January, 2011.

5

Conclusion

The creation of India and Pakistan as independent states some six decades back raised the issues rooted in colonial legacy as well as historical acrimony. The region is often recognised as a high risk conflict zone because of a history of tense relations due to border clashes and limited or large scale wars between these two neighbours. India-Pakistan differences show several aspects of the historical enmity ranging from territorial disputes to water issues. The issues of Sir Creek, Siachen Glacier and Wullar Barrage etc., are the thorny issues in bilateral relations. The future of the state of Jammu and Kashmir has been a highly contentious issue between India and Pakistan from the very time these two states gained their independence. The two states have fought three major wars (1948, 1965 and 1971) out of which two had their origins in the Kashmir dispute (1948 and 1965). This is why, the problem of Kashmir dispute is the base of differences and any hope for peace and security in South Asia lies in the solution of this issue. Despite various efforts, both India and Pakistan have failed to resolve this issue.

Although, India and Pakistan were successful in resolving the Indus Water dispute in 1960 and the Rann of Kutch dispute in 1968 through negotiations, but there was no agreed mechanism to navigate their enduring conflictual relationship. In the 1980's the two sides began to confer on the Siachen, Sir Creek and the Wullar Barrage disputes and put in place a series of confidence building measures (CBMs) pertaining to conventional and nuclear weapons. These negotiations had no set time table and were held on need-to-meet basis. A 'peace process', to be worth the name, implies existence of a structure, continuity and some understanding, however, vague of the result it seeks to achieve. In the 62 years of their existence as independent states, India and Pakistan took 50 years — half a century —to develop a process in 1997, and an unsteady one at that. Only since 2004, the peace process has become organised, acquired speed and continuity, and an agreement on the fundamentals has seemed within reach.

It was in May 1997, at Male, the capital of Maldives, the then Indian Prime Minister Inder Kumar Gujral and his Pakistani counterpart Nawaz Sharif mooted the idea of a structured dialogue or the Composite Dialogue Process. Based on a compromise approach, the peace process enabled the two countries to discuss all issues including Jammu and Kashmir, simultaneously. It was a compromise in the sense that while India agreed to include Kashmir in the agenda for talks, Pakistan relented to include terrorism, the two major irritants in bilateral relations. This first attempt at composite dialogue collapsed under the impact of the Kargil war in 1999. Although the two rounds of talks in 1998 (16–18 October and 5–13 November) had not seemed particularly propitious, the Lahore summit that followed seemed to have produced a breakthrough. However, no negotiations were likely to be able to survive the subsequent war and recriminations. From that point, the possibilities of a composite dialogue seemed distant as the Nawaz Sharif's government in Pakistan was overthrown by a military coup and the new leader, General Pervez Musharraf, condemned the Lahore summit for allowing India, in effect, to avoid addressing the violence in Kashmir. To the Indians, therefore, Pakistan seemed to be talking about the need for a Kashmir dialogue alone, and that was against the essence of the arrangement that had led to the establishment of a composite dialogue.

Following Kargil and failed Agra summit, the prospects for negotiation got much worse due to the December 13, 2001 terrorist attack on the Indian parliament. Many in India believed that Pakistan had been complicit in these actions. But that event, along with 9/11 in the United States, also restructured international politics on the subcontinent. The Taliban, supported by Pakistan, were now enemies of the United States. Americans began to look questioningly at Pakistan. Tensions rose throughout the spring and summer of 2002, as war between India and Pakistan seemed increasingly likely. Yet that tension began to diminish in October, 2002 and within six months, focus had returned to the composite dialogue. So in April, 2003, India began what was described as a 'step-by-step' initiative towards Pakistan. In July, 2003, diplomatic relations and direct transport links were re-established and in November a ceasefire was initiated. A clear opportunity for a new start was provided by the January, 2004 summit of the South Asian Association for Regional Cooperation (SAARC), and so in the last few months of 2003 and the first weeks of 2004 both sides worked hard at creating a framework that would allow for the composite dialogue to be formally revived. So, the Composite Dialogue Process was revived in June, 2004 in pursuance of a decision taken during the visit of former Prime Minister of India, Shri Atal Bihari Vajpayee to Pakistan in January, 2004. Since then, four rounds of serious discussions have taken place between India and Pakistan on eight issues in order to try and resolve all of their outstanding and contentious issues to the satisfaction of both sides. The eight issues being discussed in the composite dialogue are: peace and security, including confidence-building measures (CBMs); Jammu and Kashmir; Siachen Glacier; the Wullar Barrage/Tulbul Navigation project; Sir Creek; terrorism and drug trafficking; economic and commercial cooperation; and, the promotion of friendly exchanges. At the conclusion of the fourth round, which was delayed due to political events in Pakistan, dates for the fifth round of the Composite Dialogue were announced for July, 2008.

The fifth round of the Composite Dialogue began in July 2008. Speaking before the start of this round, Pakistan's Foreign Minister, Makhdoom Shah Mehmood Qureshi believed that the early resolution of the Siachen Glacier and Sir Creek issues was 'doable', provided that there was the political will for their expeditious resolution. On the night of the Mumbai terror attacks of November 26, 2008, just an hour before the attackers fired the first shot, the Indian and Pakistani Foreign Ministers were holding a press conference in New Delhi. The tension between the two countries at the time was over the Indian cricket team's hesitation to go play a series in Pakistan after the Marriott hotel bombing in Islamabad. Coincidentally, India's Home Secretary was in Islamabad, where the two countries had issued a comprehensive Joint Statement on fighting Terror and Drug Trafficking. India and Pakistan had agreed to 'fast-track' the fifthth round of the Composite Dialogue. Hours later all dialogue was suspended, and history was written once again by the terrorist's gun.

The fact remains that India-Pakistan relationship has been and rather remains diabolical. There are limited people-to-people contacts that may contribute to overcoming the negative perceptions that many Indians and Pakistanis have for each other. Most contacts other than family reunion are restricted to members of a small, middle-to-upper class elite prepared to endure the demanding visa and entry regimes. Indians and Pakistanis also have limited and difficult ways of accessing one another, with few flights each week between the two nations and even fewer border crossing points along their long border. There is one road crossing (Wagah-Attari) and two rail crossings (Wagah-Attari and Munabao-Khokrapar). The two nations also have very little direct trade, with Pakistan still refusing to grant India 'Most Favoured Nation' status as Islamabad claims that the balance of trade is heavily tilted in India's favour. Nevertheless, the Composite Dialogue shows that India-Pakistan relations are advancing slowly, although it seems unlikely that there will be any groundbreaking agreements in the short-to medium-term.

Besides, India and Pakistan seem to have different approaches to the Composite Dialogue. For Pakistan, its desire appears to be to get India to agree as soon as possible to resolutions to some of the serious issues that have bedeviled the India-Pakistan relationship. This desire appears to continue General Musharraf's commando style of rapid, focused, 'capture the mountain' and 'take-no-prisoners' type of diplomacy. But it also reflects Islamabad's desire and need to achieve something concrete, given the significant compromise that Pakistan made by renouncing its long-held stance to resolve the 'unfinished business of partition', the Kashmir dispute, as a prerequisite to entering into a more involved and complex relationship with India. For India, the idea seems to be to 'hasten slowly' and build up strong economic links. This, arguably, has always been India's stance, although New Delhi also has compromised by agreeing to actually discuss the Kashmir dispute in a meaningful way as part of the India-Pakistan Composite Dialogue.

The biggest problem between India and Pakistan currently is the absence of trust. Anything that addresses this trust deficit is, therefore, helpful in the way forward. In this regard let me recall what former Indian Prime Minister Vajpayee had said during a debate in the Lok Sabha: "you can change history but not geography." Prime Minister Manmohan Singh echoed similar sentiments in a debate in the Lok Sabha, where he said: "As neighbours it is our obligation to keep our channels open. Unless we want to go to war with Pakistan, dialogue is the only way forward." In this situation of distrust, the political leadership in the two countries should show political will to resolve the outstanding issues.

The Indo-Pak composite dialogue is a desirable approach but is prone to derailment if attempts are made to find instant solutions to old and complex problems. There is no alternative to an incremental peace process through political, economic and military confidence building measures. Dramatic gestures or a few summit meetings between top leaders cannot bring peace, which is only possible incrementally. India and Pakistan have a long way to go before they can resolve their major problems. The main achievements of the composite dialogue process have been in the area of CBMs designed to enhance India-Pakistan contacts and connectivity. Many such CBMs were put in place even before the commencement of the dialogue process. However, it has helped to attenuate India-Pakistan tensions by restoring snapped links and in upgrading them, enhancing people-to-people contacts and providing an institutional mechanism for the two sides to discuss their differences. It has also improved the international rating of the two countries. It needs recognition that the dialogue process has not succeeded in resolving any of the major issues in dispute like Jammu and Kashmir, Siachen, Tulbul, Sir Creek and grant of the 'Most Favoured Nation' status to India. Progress on these essential issues has been thwarted by the unreasonable positions and mutual distrust of one another. The success of the composite dialogue process depends entirely on the importance both states give to it. Regardless of how contentious the issues may be, so long as the participants are determined to remain engaged and work sincerely together, the process will bear fruit. However, in the circumstances that either side is not sincere, the process will not succeed and this situation, unless addressed seriously by governments on both sides, will no longer restore "business as usual."

The former Indian diplomat and staunch advocate of Indo-Pak amity Mr Mani Shankar Aiyar sensibly holds that there are compelling reasons why India should pro-actively engage with Pakistan. First, a tension-free relationship with Pakistan would help India to consolidate its nationhood, the bonding adhesive of which is secularism. Second, the issue of terrorism can be effectively tackled only in cooperation with Pakistan and not in confrontation with it. Third, India will not be able to play its due role in international affairs so long as it is dragged down by its quarrels with Pakistan.

Equally, is it in Pakistan's interest to seek accommodation with India for three counterpart reasons. First, the Indian bogey has harmed rather than helped consolidate the nationhood of Pakistan. Second, Pakistan is unable to become a full-fledged democracy and a sustained fast-growing economy owing to the disproportionate role assigned to alleged Indian hostility in the national affairs of the country. And, third, on the international stage, Pakistan is one of the biggest countries in the world and instead of being the front-line in someone else's war perhaps deserves to come into its own as the frontline state in the pursuit of its own interests.

APPENDIX–I

The Lahore Declaration
Signed: 21 February, 1999

The following is the text of the Lahore Declaration signed by the Prime Minister, Mr. A.B. Vajpayee, and the Pakistan Prime Minister, Mr. Nawaz Sharif, in Lahore on Sunday:

The Prime Ministers of the Republic of India and the Islamic Republic of Pakistan:

Sharing a vision of peace and stability between their countries, and of progress and prosperity for their peoples;

Convinced that durable peace and development of harmonious relations and friendly cooperation will serve the vital interests of the peoples of the two countries, enabling them to devote their energies for a better future;

Recognising that the nuclear dimension of the security environment of the two countries adds to their responsibility for avoidance of conflict between the two countries;

Committed to the principles and purposes of the Charter of the United Nations, and the universally accepted principles of peaceful coexistence;

Reiterating the determination of both countries to implementing the Simla Agreement in letter and spirit;

Committed to the objective of universal nuclear disarmament and non-proliferation;

Convinced of the importance of mutually agreed confidence building measures for improving the security environment;

Recalling their agreement of 23rd September, 1998, that an environment of peace and security is in the supreme national interest of both sides and that the resolution of all outstanding issues, including Jammu and Kashmir, is essential for this purpose.

Have agreed that their respective Governments:

- Shall intensify their efforts to resolve all issues, including the issue of Jammu and Kashmir.
- Shall refrain from intervention and interference in each other's internal affairs.
- Shall intensify their composite and integrated dialogue process for an early and positive outcome of the agreed bilateral agenda.
- Shall take immediate steps for reducing the risk of accidental or unauthorised use of nuclear weapons and discuss concepts and doctrines with a view to elaborating measures for confidence building in the nuclear and conventional fields, aimed at prevention of conflict.
- Reaffirm their commitment to the goals and objectives of SAARC and to concert their efforts towards the realisation of the SAARC vision for the year 2000 and beyond with a view to promoting the welfare of the peoples of South Asia and to improve their quality of life through accelerated economic growth, social progress and cultural development.
- Reaffirm their condemnation of terrorism in all its forms and manifestations and their determination to combat this menace.
- Shall promote and protect all human rights and fundamental freedoms.

Atal Behari Vajpayee - Prime Minister of the
Republic of India

Muhammad Nawaz Sharif - Prime Minister of the
Islamic Republic of Pakistan

APPENDIX–II

India-Pakistan Joint Press Statement, Islamabad January 06, 2004

The President of Pakistan General Pervez Musharraf and the Prime Minister of India Shri Atal Behari Vajpayee met during the SAARC summit in Islamabad.

The Indian Prime Minister while expressing satisfaction over the successful conclusion of the SAARC summit appreciated the excellent arrangements made by the host country.

Both leaders welcomed the recent steps towards normalisation of relations between the two countries and expressed the hope that the positive trends set by the CBMs would be consolidated.

Prime Minister Vajpayee said that in order to take forward and sustain the dialogue process, violence, hostility and terrorism must be prevented. President Musharraf reassured Prime Minister Vajpayee that he will not permit any territory under Pakistan's control to be used to support terrorism in any manner. President Musharraf emphasised that a sustained and productive dialogue addressing all issues would lead to positive results.

To carry the process of normalisation forward, the president of Pakistan and the Prime Minister of India agreed to commence the process of the composite dialogue in February, 2004. The two leaders are confident that the resumption of the composite dialogue will lead to peaceful settlement of all bilateral issues, including Jammu and Kashmir, to the satisfaction of both sides.

The two leaders agreed that constructive dialogue would promote progress towards the common objective of peace, security and economic development for our peoples and for future generations.

Islamabad

January 6, 2004

APPENDIX–III

Joint Statement
Sharm-el-Sheikh, July 16, 2009

The Prime Minister of India Dr. Manmohan Singh and the Prime Minister of Pakistan Syed Yusuf Raza Gilani met in Sharm El Sheikh on July 16, 2009.

The two Prime Ministers had a cordial and constructive meeting. They considered the entire gamut of bilateral relations with a view to charting the way forward in India-Pakistan relations.

Both leaders agreed that terrorism is the main threat to both countries. Both leaders affirmed their resolve to fight terrorism and to cooperate with each other to this end.

Prime Minister Singh reiterated the need to bring the perpetrators of the Mumbai attacks to justice. Prime Minister Gilani assured that Pakistan will do everything in its power in this regard. He said that Pakistan has provided an updated status dossier on the investigations of the Mumbai attacks and had sought additional information/evidence. Prime Minister Singh said that the dossier is being reviewed.

Both leaders agreed that the two countries will share real time, credible and actionable information on any future terrorist threats.

Prime Minister Gilani mentioned that Pakistan has some information on threats in Balochistan and other areas.

Both Prime Ministers recognised that dialogue is the only way forward. Action on terrorism should not be linked to the Composite Dialogue process and these should not be bracketed. Prime Minister Singh said that India was ready to discuss all issues with Pakistan, including all outstanding issues.

Prime Minister Singh reiterated India's interest in a stable, democratic, Islamic Republic of Pakistan.

Both leaders agreed that the real challenge is development and the elimination of poverty. Both leaders are resolved to eliminate those factors which prevent our countries from realising their full potential. Both agreed to work to create an atmosphere of mutual trust and confidence.

Both leaders reaffirmed their intention to promote regional cooperation.

Both Foreign Secretaries should meet as often as necessary and report to the two Foreign Ministers who will be meeting on the sidelines of the forthcoming UN General Assembly.

APPENDIX–IV

Joint Statement
September 08, 2012, Islamabad

1. The Minister of Foreign Affairs of Pakistan H.E. Ms Hina Rabbani Khar and the Minister of External Affairs of India H.E. Mr S.M. Krishna met in Islamabad on September 8, 2012, for a meeting to review progress in the Dialogue process.
2. The Ministerial level talks were preceded by a meeting between the Foreign Secretaries of Pakistan and India on September 7, 2012.
3. The talks were held in a cordial, candid and constructive atmosphere.
4. The Ministers reviewed the status of bilateral relations and expressed satisfaction on the holding of meetings on the issues of Counter-Terrorism (including progress on Mumbai trial) and Narcotics Control; Humanitarian issues; Commercial and Economic cooperation; Wullar Barrage/Tulbul Navigation Project; Sir Creek; Siachen; Peace and Security including CBMs; Jammu and Kashmir; and promotion of Friendly Exchanges.
5. The Ministers noted that the dialogue process is guided by the commitment of leadership of the two countries, expressed at the highest level, to find peaceful and mutually acceptable solutions to all outstanding issues and to build a relationship of trust and all round cooperation between Pakistan and India.
6. The Ministers expressed satisfaction at the increase in high level bilateral exchanges between the two countries since their last

meeting in New Delhi in July 2011, namely, leadership level meetings between President Asif Ali Zardari and Prime Minister Manmohan Singh at New Delhi and Tehran in April and August 2012, the first ever bilateral visit of the Speaker of Lok Sabha to Pakistan at the invitation of the Speaker of the National Assembly of Pakistan, visit of the Commerce Minister of Pakistan to India, after 35 years, in September 2011, another visit by the Commerce Minister of Pakistan to India in April 2012, and the first ever bilateral visit of the Commerce and Industry Minister of India to Pakistan in February 2012. The Ministers underlined the importance of continued high level exchange between the two countries.

7. The Ministers held substantive discussions on the whole range of issues within the framework of the Dialogue process and expressed satisfaction over the progress achieved since their last review meeting in July, 2011.
8. The Ministers reaffirmed the importance of carrying forward the dialogue process with a view to resolving peacefully all outstanding issues through constructive and result oriented engagement, and to establish friendly, cooperative and good neighbourly relations between Pakistan and India.
9. The Ministers agreed that terrorism poses a continuing threat to peace and security. They reaffirmed the strong commitment of the two countries to fight terrorism in an effective and comprehensive manner so as to eliminate the scourge in all its forms and manifestations.
10. The Ministers noted the commitment given by Pakistan during the Interior/Home Secretary talks in May 2012 to bring all the perpetrators of the Mumbai terror attacks to justice expeditiously in accordance with due process of law.
11. The Ministers noted that during the Interior/Home Secretary talks in May 2012 Indian side had conveyed that the investigation in the Samjhauta Express blast case is still ongoing and updated information will be shared with the Pakistan authorities, through diplomatic channels when the investigation is completed.
12. The Ministers welcomed the signing of the Memorandum of Understanding on "Drug Demand Reduction and Prevention of

Illicit Trafficking in Narcotics Drugs/Psychotropic Substances and Precursor Chemicals and related matters" between the Anti-Narcotics Force of Pakistan and Narcotics Control Bureau of India in September 2011 and expressed the hope that the MoU will help enhance mutual cooperation between Pakistan and India through effective and sustained steps to control the growing menace of drug trafficking.

13. The Ministers welcomed the release of prisoners and fishermen, including those suffering from ailments, in the past year or so. They agreed that the Agreement on Consular Access should be implemented in letter and spirit including immediate notification of arrests by either side, consular access to all persons within three months of arrests, release of prisoners within one month of completion of sentence and confirmation of their national status. The Ministers also welcomed the continued work of the Judicial Committee and agreed with the need to implement its recommendations on various aspects of release and repatriation of prisoners and fishermen of each country by the other and adoption of the humane approach in dealing with cases of fishermen and prisoners, especially women, elderly, juvenile, and those terminally ill or suffering from serious illness or physical/mental disability.
14. The Ministers noted that talks were held between the Director General of the Pakistan Maritime Security Agency and the Director General of the Indian Coast Guard in New Delhi in July 2012 and agreed to the importance of continuing their meetings. They further directed that the issues relating to fishermen as contained in para-10 of the Joint Statement issued after the Interior/Home Secretaries talks between Pakistan and India in March 2011 would be further examined by the relevant authorities of the two countries.
15. The Ministers welcomed the decision during the last meeting of the Home/Interior Secretaries of the two countries in May 2012 to initiate discussions in order to strengthen mutual cooperation in criminal matters.
16. The Ministers attached importance to promoting Peace and Security, including Confidence Building Measures, between the

two countries and agreed to convene separate meetings of the Expert Groups on Nuclear and Conventional CBMs, in New Delhi in the second half of December, 2012.

17. The Ministers held discussions on the issue of Jammu and Kashmir and agreed to the need for continued discussions, in a purposeful and forward looking manner, with a view to finding a peaceful solution by narrowing divergences and building convergences.

18. The Ministers reviewed the existing Cross-LoC CBMs and acknowledged that the ceasefire was holding since 2003. They also reviewed the implementation of the decisions taken regarding travel and trade across the Line of Control (LoC) in their last meeting in July 2011. They expressed satisfaction at the increasing number of people of Jammu and Kashmir who are able to avail of the facility to travel across LoC, and also at the growing Cross-LoC trade benefitting them on both sides of the LoC. They also welcomed the enhancement of the number of days for conducting trade across LoC from two to four per week, as had been agreed by them. Taking note of the recommendations made by the Joint Working Group (JWG) on Cross-LoC CBMs in its meeting in Islamabad on July 19, 2012, the Ministers decided the following:

Cross-LoC Travel

(i) Cross-LoC travel would be expanded on both sides of LoC to include visits for tourism and religious pilgrimage.

(ii) Tourist and Pilgrimage sites will be designated on both sides of the LoC and information will be available with the designated authorities.

(iii) Such visits will be conducted by designated Tour Operators in groups not exceeding 15 persons.

(iv) Permits for such visits will be single entry, non-extendable and valid for up to 15 days.

(v) Travel for tourism or pilgrimage will be arranged during summer season, i.e., April to October.

(vi) Crossing for such visits will initially be from Chakothi-Uri and Rawalakot-Poonch Crossing points.

(vii) Both sides will facilitate speedy clearance of applications for travel across LoC. The process time should not be more than 45 days.

(viii) Both sides will extend necessary assistance to valid entry permit holders to cross the LoC in emergency situation on crossing as well as non-crossing days. This will be facilitated by designated authorities.

Cross-LoC Trade

(i) List of 21 products of permissible items for Cross-LoC trade will be respected by both sides.

(ii) Regular meetings between the traders on monthly basis on both sides will be facilitated.

(iii) The designated authorities will resolve operational issues concerning Cross-LoC trade through regular meetings.

(iv) Improvement of roads and bridges for Cross-LoC trade will be facilitated.

(v) Transportation links on operational crossing points will be upgraded.

(vi) Both sides agreed to facilitate the exchange of business delegations.

19. It was agreed that the JWG on Cross-LoC CBMs will meet on a bi-annual basis to review existing arrangements and suggest additional CBMs and measures for Cross-LoC travel and trade.

20. Both sides agreed to the need for promoting friendly exchanges between the two countries. They also discussed measures for promoting cooperation in various fields including facilitating visits to religious shrines, media exchanges, holding of sports tournaments and cessation of hostile propaganda against each other.

21. The Ministers welcomed the signing of the new Visa Agreement which liberalises bilateral visa regime and introduces a number of measures aimed at easing travel of business persons, tourists, pilgrims, elderly and children, thereby facilitating contacts between peoples of the two countries, who should remain at the heart of the relationship between Pakistan and India.

22. The Ministers welcomed the signing of the Memorandum of Understanding on cooperation in the field of culture between the Pakistan National Council of the Arts and the Indian Council for Cultural Relations.

23. The two sides exchanged views on Siachen, Sir Creek and Wullar Barrage/Tulbul Navigation Project, agreed that there is the need to effectively address these issues by finding mutually acceptable solutions and reiterated their commitment to do so. They also reaffirmed the importance of abiding by the provisions of the Indus Waters Treaty.

24. The Ministers expressed satisfaction at the progress registered towards normalising bilateral trade and commercial relations. The Ministers firmly reiterated that both sides will scrupulously adhere to the roadmap drawn up by the two Commerce Ministries for full normalisation of trade relations. They agreed that a strong and enhanced economic partnership is in the interest of peoples of both countries.

25. The Ministers welcomed reactivation of the Pakistan-India Joint Commission, in accordance with their decision taken last year. They Co-chaired the Plenary of the Joint Commission, which met for the first time after 2007. They expressed satisfaction at the meetings of all eight Technical Level Working Groups and noted that these Groups have made a number of suggestions for exploring mutually beneficial cooperation in areas of agriculture, education, environment, health, information and broadcasting, information technology and telecommunication, science and technology and tourism. They took note of and approved the Report by the Foreign Secretaries, which is annexed.

26. The Ministers reaffirmed their commitment to the goals and objectives of SAARC and agreed to make joint efforts to promote cooperation for regional development in the SAARC framework.

27. The Ministers agreed to the launch of the next round of Secretary level dialogue on all eight segments, as contained in para-4 above. Schedule for these meetings will be worked out through diplomatic channels. They further agreed that all these meetings will be held prior to their next review meeting in New Delhi in 2013.

28. The External Affairs Minister of India called on the President and the Prime Minister of Pakistan.

Areas Identified for Cooperation by Technical Level Working Groups of the Pakistan-India Joint Commission

- The Pakistan-India Joint Commission met in Islamabad on 6th September, 2012 in pursuance of the decision taken by the Minister of Foreign Affairs of Pakistan and Minister of External Affairs of India during their last meeting in New Delhi on 27th July 2011. The reactivation of the Joint Commission was welcomed by both sides. The following eight Technical Level Working Groups (TLWG) discussed and identified avenues of mutually beneficial cooperation in the respective fields:
    - Agriculture
    - Education
    - Environment
    - Health
    - Information
    - IT & Telecom
    - Science and Technology
    - Tourism.
- The working group on Agriculture discussed avenues of cooperation and identified certain areas for collaboration including exchange of experts and training of scientists in the areas of crop improvement through the use of biotechnology, cooperation in seed sector, quarantine related matters, livestock and dairy development sector, high efficiency irrigation system and rain water harvesting.
- The working group on Education explored avenues for furthering cooperation in the fields of school and higher education, non-formal education and adult literacy. It also explored furthering cooperation through institutional linkages between Higher Education Commission of Pakistan and University Grants Commission of India, linkages between National Vocational and Technical Training Commission of Pakistan and All India Council

for Technical Education of India and exchange of experiences between National Book Foundation of Pakistan, National Book Trust and National Council of Educational Research and Training of India.

- The working group on Environment discussed various issues relating to environment and agreed to enhance cooperation in the fields of climate change, renewable energy, environmental protection, energy conservation and Clean Development Mechanism, Bio-diversity and sustainable forest conservation, solid waste management. It agreed to share experiences and best practices including establishing institutional linkages for knowledge sharing and capacity building.
- The working group on Health agreed to enhance cooperation in polio eradication and increasing immunisation coverage, cooperation in women and child health, sharing experience for retaining human resourses in rural area exchange of information on regulatory regime and institutional collaboration between Drug Regulatory Agency of Pakistan and Central Drugs Standard Control Organisation of India. They also agreed to enhance cooperation in Quality Assurance and Drug Testing laboratories in pharmaceuticals and biological.
- The working group on Information discussed issues concerning Information and Broadcasting. In this context, exchange of journalists and information professionals, organising film festivals in each other's countries, holding of seminars/workshops, between Indian Institute of Mass Communication (IIMC) and suitable Pakistani Institute; and between Film and Television Institute of India(FTII) and Academies of Pakistan Television Corporation and Pakistan Broadcasting Corporation; news exchange between official news agencies and exchange of TV and Radio programmes were identified for future collaboration. Both sides agreed that media can play a pivotal role in building and enabling environment between the two countries.
- The Working group on IT and Telecom discussed avenues of cooperation. Pakistan invited Indian companies to participate in ICT events in Pakistan. India offered to organise a customised

e-governance workshop in India for Pakistan. They also discussed possibilities of collaboration in International Domain Name (IDN), sharing best practices on e-governance. Open Source Technologies and IT Enabled Services. The Group emphasised improved visa facilitation for IT & Telecom professionals. India offered to forward a proposal for establishing telemedicine linkages between the two countries.

- The working group on Science and Technology discussed National Science, Technology Innovation System in Pakistan and India. They agreed to work on common areas of interest by holding joint workshops/seminars and short training programmes. They identified areas of medicinal plants and herbal medicines (in Pakistan), renewable energy (in India) and Standards for such collaboration. Both sides also agreed to participate in each other's science popularisation programmes /activities.
- The working group on Tourism held discussion on tourism industry and potential in both countries. They explored and identified areas for cooperation particularly in information sharing, Research and Development, human resource development in the field of tourism, Destination management, marketing and promotion, Meetings Incentives Conference and Exhibition (MICE) tourism, travel and hospitality industry.

Bibliography

Primary Sources

1. Debates in the UN.
2. The Jammu and Kashmir Assembly Debates.
3. Debates in SAARC Summits.
4. Indian Parliamentary Debates.
5. Interviews.
6. Ministry of External Affairs (India), Annual Reports.
7. Ministry of Foreign Relations (Pakistan), Annual Reports.
8. National Manifestoes of Political Parties in India and Pakistan.
9. Pakistani Parliamentary Debates.
10. United Nations Year Books.
11. White Paper on Jammu and Kashmir, Government of India (1948).

Secondary Sources

Books

Abdullah Farooq, *My Dismissal,* Vikas, New Delhi, 1985.

Abdullah Sheikh Mohammad, *Flames of the Chinar: An Autobiography,* English translation by Khushwant Singh, Viking, New Delhi, 1993.

Advani, L.K., *My Country, My Life,* Rupa and Co., New Delhi, 2008.

Agha Ayesha Siddiqa, *Pakistan's Arms Procurement and Military Build-up, 1979-99: In search of a policy,* Palgrave, 2001.

Ahmar Moonis, *Internal and External Dynamics of South Asian Security,* Fazeelsons, Karachi, 2001.

—— *The Challenge of Confidence-Building in South Asia,* Har-Anand Publications, New Delhi, 2001.

Ahmed Zahid Shahab and Balasubramanian Rajeshwari, *Extremism in Pakistan and India: The Case of the Jamaat-e-Islami and Shiv Sena,* Regional Centre for Strategic Studies (RCSS), Colombo, 2010.

Aiyar Mani Shankar, *Pakistan papers,* UBS Publishers, New Delhi, 1994.

Akbar, M.J., *Kashmir: Behind the Vale,* Viking Penguin, New Delhi, 1991.

Anand, A.S, *The Constitution of Jammu and Kashmir: Its Development and Comments,* Universal Law Publishing Co., New Delhi, 1990.

Bajpai, Kanti, Chari P.R., Cheema PervaizIqbal, Cohen Stephen Pand Ganguly Sumit, *Brasstacks and Beyond: Perception and Management of Crisis in South Asia*, Manohar, New Delhi, 1995.

Bajpai Kanti, Karim Afsir, Mattoo Amitabh, *Kargil and After: Challenges for Indian Policy,* Har-Anand Publications, New Delhi, 2001.

Bakshi, S.R., *Kashmir Through Ages*, Vol. 5, Sarup and Sons, New Delhi, 1997.

Banerji Dipankar, *Confidence Building Measures in South Asia,* Regional Centre for Strategic Studies (RCSS), Colombo, 1999.

Bazaz Prem Nath, *Kashmir in Crucible,* Pamposh, New Delhi, 1967.

—— *The History of Struggle for Freedom in Kashmir: Cultural and Political,* Kashmir Publishing Company, New Delhi, 1954.

Behera Navnita Chadha, *Demystifying Kashmir,* Brookings Institution, Washington DC, 2006.

Bhasin Avtar Singh, *India's Foreign Relations – 2005 Documents*, Geetika Publishers, New Delhi, 2005.

Bhattacharjea Ajit, *Kashmir: The Wounded Valley,* UBSPD, New Delhi, 1994.

Bhutto Benazir, *Reconciliation: Islam, Democracy, and the West,* HarperCollins, New York, 2008.

Bidwai Praful and Vanaik Achin, *New Nukes: India, Pakistan and Global Nuclear Disarmament,* Interlink Books, New York, 2000.

Bindra, S.S., *Indo-Pak Relations: Tashkent to Simla Agreement,* Deep and Deep Publications, New Delhi, 1981.

Boquérat Gilles and Asbeck Richard, *The India-Pakistan Reconciliation and Other Experiences in Post-Conflict Management,* The Institut Français des Relations Internationales (IFRI), Paris, 2009.

Bose Sumantra, *Kashmir: Roots of Conflict, Paths to Peace,* Vistaar Publications, New Delhi, 2003.

Burke, S.M. and Ziring Lawrençe, *Pakistan's Foreign Policy: An Historical Analysis* (second edition), Oxford University Press, Karachi, 1990.

Burke, S.M., *Mainsprings of Indian and Pakistani Foreign Policies,* Minneapolis: University of Minnesota Press, 1974.

Chandran Suba, Zeb Rizwan, *Taking the Indo-Pak Peace Process Further,* IPCS Policy Brief 2, March 2004.

Chari, P.R., Cheema Pervaiz Iqbal, *The Simla Agreement 1972: Its Wasted Promise,* Manohar Publishers, New Delhi, 2001.

Cohen Stephen Philip, *The Idea of Pakistan,* Oxford University Press, New Delhi, 2004.

—— *The Structural Dimensions of Conflict in South Asia,* Regional Centre for Strategic Studies (RCSS), Colombo, 1997.

Dixit, J.N., *India-Pakistan in War and Peace,* Ashok Chopra, Book Today, New Delhi, 2002.

Durrani Mahmud Ali, *India and Pakistan: The Cost of Conflict and the Benefits of Peace,* Oxford University Press, Karachi, 2001.

Dutt, V.P., *India's Foreign Policy,* Viking Publishing House, New Delhi, 1984.

Evans Paul M, Rizvi Gowher, Behera Navnita C., *Beyond Boundaries: A Report on the State of Non-Official Dialogues on Peace, Security and Cooperation in South Asia,* University of Toronto/York University, Ontario, 1997.

Faiz Asma-ul-Husna, *India Pakistan Dialogue: Bringing the Society in,* Regional Centre for Strategic Studies (RCSS), Colombo, 2007.

Ganguly Sumit, *The Crisis in Kashmir: Portents of War, Hopes of Peace,* Cambridge University Press, Cambridge, 1997.

Ghuman, R.S., *Indo-Pakistan Trade Relations,* Deep and Deep Publications, New Delhi, 1986.

Gilani Syed Ali, *Nawaiy Hurriyat* (Urdu), Institute of Policy Studies, Islamabad, 1994.

Graham, B.D., *Hindu Nationalism and Indian Politics: The Origins and Development of the Bharatiya Jana Sangh,* Cambridge University Press, Cambridge, 1990.

Gupta, K.R., *India-Pakistan Relations with Special Reference to Kashmir,* Atlantic Publishers and Distributors, New Delhi, 2003.

Gupta Sisir, *Kashmir: A Study in India-Pakistan Relations,* Asia Publishing House, Bombay, 1996.

Harrison Selig S., Kreisberg Paul H., and Kux Dennis, *India and Pakistan: The first fifty years,* Cambridge University Press, Cambridge, 1999.

Hasan Mushirul, *India's Partition: Process, Strategy and Mobilisation*, Oxford University Press, New Delhi, 1993.

Jalal Ayesha, *The State of Martial Rule: The origins of Pakistan's political economy of defence,* Cambridge University Press, Cambridge, 1990.

—— *Democracy and Authoritarianism in South Asia: A comparative and historical perspective*, Cambridge University Press, Cambridge, 1995.

Jha Prem Shankar, *Kashmir 1947: Rival Versions of History,* Oxford University Press, Delhi, 1996.

Khan, M. Asghar, *Pakistan: Politics and Military Power,* Oxford University Press, Karachi, 2005.

Khanna, D.D., Kumar Kishore, *Dialogue of the Deaf: The India-Pakistan Divide,* Konark Publishers, Delhi, 1992.

Khanna, V.N., *Foreign Policy of India,* Vikas Publishing House, New Delhi, 2001.

Kohli Atul, *Democracy and Discontent: India's Growing Crisis of Governability*, Cambridge University Press, Cambridge, 1990.

Kumar, D.P, *Kashmir: Return to Democracy,* Siddhi Books, New Delhi, 1996.

Kumar Rajesh, *Getting To Rapprochement Over Kashmir: Is Using the 'China Model' a Viable Alternative,* RCSS, Colombo, Sir Lanka, 2007.

Lamb Alastair, *A Disputed Legacy 1846-1990,* Oxford University Press, Pakistan, 1991.

——— *Birth of a Tragedy: Kashmir 1947*, Oxford University Press, Karachi, 1994.

Lt. Gen. Raghavan, V.R., *Siachen: Conflict without End,* Viking Penguin Books India, New Delhi, 2002.

Malhotra Jagmohan, *My Frozen Turbulence in Kashmir,* Allied, New Delhi, 1994.

Malik Iffat, *Kashmir: Ethnic Conflict, International Dispute,* Oxford University Press, 2005.

Mathur Alok, *The Two Nation Theory: A study in the Context of Identity Crisis in Pakistan,* Aalekh Publishers, Jaipur, India, 1994.

Mattoo Amitabh, Kak Kapil, Jacob Happymon. *India and Pakistan: Pathways Ahead,* KW Publishers, New Delhi, 2007.

Menon Raja, *A Nuclear Strategy for India*, Sage, New Delhi, 2000.

More, D.R., *India and Pakistan: Fell Apart,* Shruti Publications, Jaipur, India, 2004.

Muni, S.D., *India's Foreign Policy: The Democracy Dimension,* Foundation Books, New Delhi, 2009.

Musharraf Pervez, *In the Line of Fire: A Memoir,* Simon and Schuster, UK, 2006.

Nayar Kuldip, *Wall at Wagah: India-Pakistan Relations,* Gyan Publishing House, New Delhi, 2003.

Nikhil Chakravartty's Writings, *India-Pakistan: Themes Beyond Borders,* Konark Publishers, Delhi, 2004.

Paul, T.V., *The India-Pakistan Conflict: An Enduring Rivalry,* Cambridge University Press, New Delhi, 2006.

Puri Balraj, *Kashmir towards Insurgency,* Orient Longman, Hyderabad, 1993.

—— *Simmering Volcano: Study of Jammu Relations with Kashmir,* Sterling, New Delhi, 1983.

Ramakant, Kaushik S.N., Upadhyaya Shashi, *Contemporary Pakistan: Trends and Issues,* (Vol. I), Kalinga Publications, Delhi, 2001.

Sareen Rajendra, *Pakistan: The Indian Factor,* Allied Publishers, New Delhi, 1984.

Schafffer Howard, *The Limits of Influence: America's Role in Kashmir,* Viking, 2009.

Schofield Victoria, *Kashmir in Conflict: India, Pakistan and the Unending War,* I.B. Tauris, London, 2003.

Sewak Manjrika, *Multi-Track Diplomacy between India and Pakistan: A Conceptual Framework for Sustainable Security,* Manohar Publishers and Distributors, New Delhi, 2005.

Singh Anita Inder, *The Origins of the Partition of India 1936-1947*, Oxford University Press, New Delhi, 1987.

Singh Gopal, *South Asia: Democracy, Discontent and Societal Conflicts*, Amamika Publishers, Delhi, 1998.

Singh Jasjit, *Kargil 1999: Pakistan's Fourth War for Kashmir,* KW Publishers, New Delhi, 1999.

Singh Jaswant, *Jinnah: India Partition Independence,* Rupa and Co., New Delhi, 2009.

Singh Karan, *Heir Apparent: An Autobiography,* Oxford University Press, Delhi, 1982.

Swami Praveen, *India, Pakistan and the Secret Jihad: The Covert War in Kashmir, 1947-2004,* Routledge, Oxon, 2007.

Tellis Ashley, Fair C., and Medby J., *Limited Conflicts Under the Nuclear Umbrella: Indian and Pakistani Lessons from the Kargil Crisis,* RAND Corporation, 2001.

Tripathy Sasmita, Rid Saeed Ahmed, *Democracy as a Conflict-Resolution Model for Terrorism: A Case Study of India and Pakistan,* Regional Centre for Strategic Studies (RCSS), Colombo, 2010.

Trivedi Ram Naresh, *Sino-Indian Border Dispute and its impact on Indo-Pak Relations,* Associated House, New Delhi, 1977.

Wani Gull Mohd, *Kashmir: from Autonomy to Azadi*, Valley Book House, Srinagar, 1996.

—— *Kashmir: Need for Sub-Continental Political Initiative,* Ashish Publishing House, New Delhi, 1995.

—— *Kashmir: Politics, Problems and Prospects,* Ashish, New Delhi, 1993.

Wirsing Robert, *Kashmir in the Shadow of War: Regional Rivalries in a Nuclear Age,* Spring Books Gurgaon, India, 2004.

—— *Kashmir: Resolving Regional Conflict,* Kartikeya Publications, Meerut (U.P.), India, 1996.

Wolpert Stanley, *A New History of India,* Oxford University Press, 2000.

—— *India and Pakistan: Continued Conflict or Cooperation?* University of California Press, California, 2010.

Yadav, Y.S., *India's Foreign Policy Towards 2000 A.D.,* Deep and Deep Publishers, New Delhi, 1993.

Zeb Rizwan, Chandran Suba, *Indo-Pak Conflicts, Ripe to Resolve?* , Regional Centre for Strategic Studies (RCSS) Colombo, Manohar Publishers and Distributors, New Delhi, 2005.

Articles:

Ahmad Samina and Sahni Varun, "Freezing the Fighting: Military Disengagement on Siachen Glacier", *Cooperative Monitoring Center Occasional Papers* (Sandia National Laboratories, Albuquerque) 1998.

Ahmed Ishtiaq, "India-Pakistan Relations: Post-Mumbai Terrorist Attacks", *Institute of South Asian Studies, (ISAS),* National University of Singapore (NUS), Insights No. 89, January 7, 2010.

Ahuja Rajesh, "Pak. must vacate occupied territory", *The Hindu*, Oct 19, 2003.

Aiyar Mani Shankar, "India-Pakistan: Retrospect and Prospect", *Wilhelm Von Pochhammer Memorial Lecture,* New Delhi, 12 January 2011.

Akhtar Shaheen, "War on Terrorism and Kashmir issue", *Institute of Regional Studies (IRS),* Islamabad, 2010.

Aneja Atul, "Reconstructing the Agra Summit," *The Hindu*, 27 July 2001.

—— "Siachen Accord Envisages a Thaw," *The Hindu*, March 28, 1997.

Baruah Amit, "India proposes a Dozen Steps to Break the Ice with Pak", *The Hindu*, 23 October 2003.

—— "The Bus to Pakistan", *Frontline*, India, March 12, 1999.

Behuria Ashok K, "India-Pakistan Relations: An Indian Narrative", *Pakistan Institute of Legislative Development and Transparency, (PILDAT)*, January 2011.

—— "Pakistan's Approach to Kashmir since the Lahore Agreement: Is There Any Change?" *Strategic Analysis*, New Delhi.

Bhushan Bharat, "Tulbul, Sir Creek and Siachen: Competitive Methodologies", *South Asian Journal*, 2005.

Borah Mridusmita, "Third Round Table Conference on Kashmir: Is there a Consensus?" *Institute of Peace and Conflict Studies*, New Delhi, # 2292, 16 May, 2007.

Cheema PervaizIqbal, "More Confidence Building Measures", *Pakistan Observer*, Oct. 13, 2007.

—— "The Contribution of Track-11 towards India-Pakistan Relations", *South Asian Survey*, New Delhi, September 2006.

Coll Steve, "The Back Channel", *The New Yorker*, March 2, 2009.

Constable Pamela, "Indian Announces One-Month Cease-Fire in Kashmir; Unilateral Move at Opening Talks With Rebel Groups," *Washington Post*, 20 November 2000.

Dobell, W.M, "Ramifications of the China-Pakistan Border Treaty", *Pacific Affairs*, Vol. 37, No. 3 (Autumn, 1964).

Fayyaz Shabana, "Indo-Pak Joint Anti-Terrorism Mechanism: Perspectives from Pakistan", *Institute of Peace and Conflict Studies (IPCS)*, Issue Brief 126, September 2009.

Ganguly Rajat, "India, Pakistan and the Kashmir insurgency: causes, dynamics and prospects for resolution", *Asian Studies Review*, Routledge, UK, 2001.

Ghosh Samarjit, "Indo-Pak Composite Dialogue—2008: A Review", *Institute of Peace and Conflict Studies (IPCS)*, New Delhi, Special Report, 65, February, 2009.

——"Two Decades of Indo-Pak CBMs: A Critique from India", *Institute of Peace and Conflict Studies,* New Delhi, Issue Brief 132, September 2009.

Ghuman Ranjit Singh, Madaan Davinder Kumar, "Indo-Pakistan Trade Cooperation and SAARC", *Peace and Democracy in South Asia,* Vol. 2, No. 1, 2006.

Gul Nabiha, "Enhancing Indo-Pak Trade: Perspectives from Pakistan", *Institute of Peace and Conflict Studies,* Issue Brief 122, New Delhi, September, 2009.

Haidar Suhasini, "India and Pakistan: deadlines for dialogue", *The Hindu,* January 12, 2010.

Harshe Rajen, "Cross-Border Terrorism: Road-Block to Peace Initiatives", *Economic and Political Weekly*, August 30, 2003.

Hersh Seymour, "On the Nuclear Edge," *The New Yorker,* March 29, 1993.

Irshad Muhammad, "Indo-Pak Confidence-Building Measures", *Defence Journal,* Karachi, August, 2002.

Joseph Mallika, "Delhi Round of Indo-Pak Talks – II: Tulbul Navigation Project/Wullar Barrage", *Islamabad Policy Research Institute (IPRI),* November 21, 1998.

Kanwal Gurmeet, "Does Siachen have Major Strategic Significance?" *Asian Tribune,* May 22, 2007.

Khan Muhammad Ejaz, "Musharraf sees foreign hand in Baluchistan unrest", *The News,* 5 August, 2008.

Khare Harish, "Kashmir: New Roadmap Taking Shape," http://www.hinduonnet.com.

Mahmood Javed, Baloch Shafi, "UN keeps mum on Sir Creek dispute", *The Nation*, September 7, 2009.

Malhotra Pia, "Enhancing Indo-Pak Trade: Perspectives from India", *Institute of Peace and Conflict Studies,* Issue Brief 119, New Delhi, September 2009.

Manjunath KS, Sridhar Seema, Anand Beryl, "Indo-Pak Composite Dialogue 2004-05: A Profile", *Institute of Peace and Conflict Studies,* New Delhi, Special Report 12, February, 2006.

Misra Ashutosh, "An audit of the India-Pakistan peace process", *Australian Journal of International Affairs,* Routledge, UK, 2007.

—— "The Sir Creek Boundary Dispute: A Victim of India-Pakistan Linkage Politics", *International Boundaries Research Unit (IBRU)*, Boundary and Security Bulletin, UK, Winter 2000-2001.

Mohan, C. Raja, "Fernandes Unveils 'Limited War' Doctrine," *The Hindu,* 25 January 2000.

Noorani, A.G., "India-Pakistan Peace Process", *Institute of Regional Studies,* Seminar Papers, Islamabad, 20-21 Oct. 2008.

—— "The Siachen impasse", *Frontline,* November 09 - 22, 2002.

Patil Sameer Suryakant, "Indo-Pak Composite Dialogue: An Update", *Institute of Peace and Conflict Studies (IPCS),* Special Report, No. 53, June 2008.

Pattanaik Smruti S., Anan Arpita, "Cross-LoC Confidence Building Measures between India and Pakistan: A Giant Leap or a Small Step towards Peace?" *Institute for Defence Studies and Analyses*, Issue Brief, February 12, 2010.

Reddy Muralidhar, "India, Pakistan seek to resolve dispute over coastal strip off Gujarat coast", *The Hindu,* May 29, 2005.

Roy Arundhati, "The End of Imagination", *The Guardian,* UK, August 1, 1998.

Sharma Kalpana, "The Hindu Bomb", *The Bulletin of the Atomic Scientists,* Chicago, USA, July 1998.

Sidju Harjinder, "Ansari Arrest Proves Pak Hand: PM," *Hindustan Times,* Feb. 11, 2002.

Snedden Christopher, "The India-Pakistan Peace Process: Overcoming the Trust Deficit", *Pakistan Security Research Unit (PSRU),* Brief Number 20, October 2, 2007.

— "The India-Pakistan Peace Process: Stronger, but with some interference", *Institute of Regional Studies (IRS),* Seminar Papers, Islamabad, 20-21 Oct. 2008.

Soherwordi Syed Hussain Shaheed, "CBMs and Peace in South Asia", *Defence Journal,* Karachi, August 2000.

Sridhar Seema, "Kashmir and Water: Conflict and Cooperation", *Programme in Arms Control, Disarmament, and International Security* (ACDIS),University of Illinois at Urbana-Champaign, 2008.

Swami Praveen, "Bits of Consensus", *Frontline,* Vol. 24, No. 9, May 5-18, 2007.

—— "Fighting Pakistan's informal war", *The Hindu,* Jul y 15, 2008.

Urfi Muhammad Arif, "Intra Kashmir Trade", *Pakistan Institute of Legislative Development and Transparency* (PILDAT), Policy Brief, January 2011.

Zeb Rizwan, "Peace Process, Spoilers and Indo-Pak Conflict", *Pak Institute for Peace Studies* (PIPS), Islamabad, Pakistan, September 29, 2009.

—— "Recent Indo-Pak Offers: Old Wine in New Bottle?" *Institute of Regional Studies,* Islamabad, #1214, 27 November 2003.

Periodicals:

1. **News Papers**
    - Asian Tribune, Bangkok, (Thailand).
    - Daily Times, Lahore, (Pakistan).
    - Dawn, Karachi, (Pakistan).
    - Friday Times, Lahore, (Pakistan).
    - Hindustan Times, New Delhi.
    - Pakistan Observer, Islamabad, (Pakistan).
    - The Financial Express, New Delhi.
    - The Guardian, UK.
    - The Hindu, Chennai.
    - The Nation, Lahore, (Pakistan).
    - The New York Times, New York.
    - The News, Karachi, (Pakistan).
    - The Statesman, Kolkata.
    - The Times of India, New Delhi.
    - The Tribune, Chandigarh.

- The Washington Post, Washington DC.
- Greater Kashmir, Srinagar.

2. **Magazines**
   - Economic and Political Weekly, Mumbai.
   - Epilogue, Jammu.
   - Frontline, Chennai.
   - Herald, Karachi, (Pakistan).
   - Himal, Kathmandu, (Nepal).
   - India Today, New Delhi.
   - Mainstream, New Delhi.
   - Outlook, New Delhi.
   - South Asia Politics, New Delhi.
   - The New Yorker, USA.
   - Third Concept, New Delhi.
3. **Journals**
   - AGNI—The Journal of the FSSS, New Delhi.
   - Aspects of India's Economy, Mumbai.
   - Australian Journal of International Affairs, Australia.
   - Defence Journal, Karachi, (Pakistan).
   - Journal of Peace and Democracy in South Asia, Stockholm, (Sweden).
   - South Asian Journal, Lahore, (Pakistan).
   - South Asian Survey, New Delhi.
   - Strategic Analysis, Institute for Defence Studies and Analyses (IDSA), New Delhi.
   - The Caravan – A Journal of Politics and Culture, New Delhi.

Websites

- www.hinduonnet.com
- www.icrier.org
- www.indembkwt.org
- www.meaindia.nic.in

- www.mofa.gov.pk
- www.ndtv.com
- www.news.bbc.co.uk
- www.satp.org
- www.siachenglacier.com
- www.stimson.org
- www.thenews.com.p
- www.tribuneindia.com
- www.un.org
- www.uvm.edu

Index